A Couple of Tea

To Betty

Happy reading!

A Couple of Tea

a creative memoir

by Ann Benattar

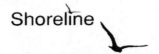

Shoreline

Cover: Paul Taylor
Graphic design: Paul Taylor,
with thanks to Sarah Robinson

Shoreline
23 Ste-Anne, Ste-Anne-de-Bellevue, QC H9X 1L1
shorelinepress@bell.net www.shorelinepress.ca
514.457.5733

Printed in Canada by Transcontinental

Dépôt legal: Library and Archives Canada
et Bibliothèque et Archives nationales du Québec

Library and Archives Canada Cataloguing in Publication

Benattar, Ann, 1927-
A couple of tea / Ann Benattar.

ISBN 978-1-896754-83-3

1. Benattar, Ann, 1927-. 2. Benattar, Henry.
3. Couples--Biography. 4. Authors, Canadian
(English)--Biography. 5. Montréal Island (Québec :
Island)--Biography. 6. Muskoka (Ont. : District
municipality)--Biography. I. Title.

HQ801.B396 2010   306.8   C2010-904446-0

Dedication

To my parents for guiding me along a good path, and for giving me a love of reading and a sense of humour. To my husband and children for their unwavering support, oft-requested assistance using their skills with computers, and their (perhaps unbeknownst to them) inspiration for many of the Backwards Boater columns and above all for believing in me.

Contents

Prologue

Sunrise Tea:
The beginning
of the story

Introducing Earl and Grace

There it is, right in the far dusty corner of our basement: the old green card table.

I squeeze past the floor-to-ceiling towers of boxes, the rusty collection of old bicycles, the books, books and (of course) more books, and finally reach it. Just running my fingers along its edge conjures up a flash of memories. So many tales, so much 'past' contained in those few inches of wood and metal. What stories that card table could tell. What stories *I* could tell *about* the card table. It stirs something within me. Now to get it upstairs.

Most of the morning has been quiet and peaceful: Henry drinking tea and reading the newspaper, while I had been planning to sit down and write some long letters to the children. Another blissful Spring day in our home in Pierrefonds. Dragging the card table upstairs from the basement threatens to burst that bubble, but it's suddenly important to me. Maybe I'm having a 'senior's moment', or perhaps there's something about the card table, all the history it has witnessed, that I hope to capture and relive. It seems such a shame for it to be lost, just a neglected piece of furniture in our dark basement.

My huffing and puffing – not to mention the racket I make hauling the table up the basement stairs – summons a holler from Henry.

"What's happening there, Annie?"

I reach the top of the stairs, lift the table through the dining room and prop it up in the kitchen, within sight of my husband.

"The old card table?" he says, lowering his newspaper. "What's that doing up here?"

"I know it's just a silly little card table, Henry, but I tell you I'd be heartbroken if thieves broke into our house and stole it! They can have the crystal, the silverware, our cameras and computer, but they can't have my green card table!" My vigour makes me lurch forward practically into my husband's lap.

"Watch it, Annie. My tea is splashing overboard," Henry declares, holding out the newspaper to protect his new pants. Bending down to look at the floor, he adds, "And you already washed the floor this morning."

"Jeepers, Henry, didn't you hear what I said?"

"Of course I did, Annie, but I don't believe what I heard. As you said yourself, 'It's a silly old card table so why the fuss?'" There is a tiny upward movement at the corners of his mouth that I only just notice. "You're full of surprises as always, dear."

After wiping the spill with a piece of paper towel, I lean against the counter and plant my feet firmly on the floor. "Now you listen to me, Henry. I am serious!" I feel two vivid red splotches flare up on my cheeks as I point at the subject of my concern resting on its side against the kitchen door.

Four folded, scratched metal legs frame the square table. I spot the name 'Boswell' written in pencil on one corner of the back of the table. "Oh, m'god, that's Mum's handwriting! I haven't seen that for years. Henry, I still miss Mum's letters, even after all this time."

"I don't blame you, Annie. Besides, seven years isn't such a long time, really."

"No, it isn't. You're lucky you still have your mother even if she does live so far away."

"Of course," says Henry. "But I really miss your mother, too, you know."

Grasping the table lovingly, I turn it around so that its lime green surface catches a patch of sunlight in the tiny kitchen. Although it is covered with a thin layer of dust after a summer of disuse, a small circular stain grabs my attention. Slowly I trace the circle with my fingertips, "I remember how this got here. Never could get it out! It was Welch's grape juice mixed with ginger ale. Mum had put it beside me when I was doing art at the table but while I was erasing my picture with that rubbery thing (art gum?), some spilled over and dribbled down the sides of the glass. I should have cleaned it right away but, heck, I was probably only six years old when that happened."

Henry reaches out and grasps my hands. With a chuckle he says, "Why do I feel another story coming on? Come and sit down." He pats the stool opposite him at the other side of the kitchen's miniature, built-in table. "Dearest, as I've told you a million times, you should write your stories down."

"For Pete's sake, Henry, you know I can't. I wasn't exactly an academic success in High School. I had a terrible inferiority complex." I get up to run some water over the dishrag I'd picked up out of the sink, give it a squeeze then lean over the card table again.

"Don't bother, dear," Henry says. "That stain will never come out."

"Oh, I know. Truth is, I rather like it. It brings back so many memories."

"Please sit down. I want to talk to you. I'll make us a couple of tea," he says, rubbing his hands together. "Now there's a good memory for you, Annie."

"What memory?"

"When four-year-old Samantha offered Nanny 'a couple of tea.'"

"Oh, that gave us such a good laugh, didn't it, Henry?" Chortling, I take another quick swipe at the table and finally sit down again. "I'm all ears, dear."

My face, ruddy from what I describe deprecatingly as my 'oven tan', looks like that of a happy, young girl. No, I do not look my age. Henry constantly tells me that. Looking at me, he says, "I don't know how you do it. You still manage to look like the beautiful young girl I married."

I blush and reply, "That's because by contrast you are silver, senatorial and sensational. Like Gregory Peck. You see, dear, I'm practising alliteration."

Almost in a whisper Henry despairs, "Thanks, dear, but I'm not tall and slim like he is."

"Yes, but handsome. You can't win them all." I laugh. "If I add sexy, I'd have four 's' words describing you!"

"Listen to me. I'm serious. You should write down all your stories. They're interesting, funny, often moving, and you do have an affinity with words."

"Really?"

"Yes, dear, when you write letters your grammar is perfect. You know about computers, even your punctuation gets corrected when you use Word. Why don't you try to write a book of short stories? You have so much to say and you're very entertaining." He slaps his hands on the table. "Do it! Maybe you could even write a newspaper column, or something like that."

"My name may be Boswell but I certainly don't have his talent."

"But the name would help you. I'm sure. It certainly can't hurt."

"Sure, and I am very proud to have James Boswell as my ancestor. I've seen his name on our family tree many times." Feeling excited, I gulp down the rest of my tea in one fell swoop. After a bout of coughing, I strike a pose. "About what would I write, pray tell?"

"About anything you want. Let me see, you can write about some of the characters in the neighbourhood, about learning to play the didgeridoo, about your fishing experiences, or mine." Smiling, he continues, "About buying the cottage and how hard it is to be an islander, for example. Or you can write about turkey disasters, or your bridge group." The latter idea produces a twinkle in his warm, molasses-coloured eyes. "You can rant and rave all you want about growing up in Toronto, about the four seasons, how you love winter, about the ducks at the cottage, about Pat's rescuing a mouse in the back yard and bestowing a kiss on the little thing only to have it bite through his lip in order to hang on. Didn't we have the worst time getting the frightened critter off him!" We erupt in laughter. "So many, many choices, my dear. You're the one with the colourful imagination!"

Looking very pleased with himself, Henry folds his arms across his chest.

"Shoot, maybe *you* should write it then! I didn't even take English at university. Oh, how I wish I had majored in English instead of French and Spanish! I just wouldn't know where to begin, Henry."

"Just write from your heart, Annie. If you like, I'll read your rough drafts for clarity, but you should not be inhibited when you write. Let it flow."

"Let it flow. Mm, that sounds easy. I like that."

"Just be your own sweet self."

"Thanks, Henry, I think I'll try. I'll write the stuff and send it to the kids. I'm not so sure about getting published, though." Doubt is already changing my mood as I look up at my husband.

"And should I use real names? What would the real people think?" I ask.

"Well, you could always change the names. Authors are always doing that. Heck, they even use pseudonyms," he says.

"So, who do you want to be? After all, you'd be a main character. What name have you always wanted? Christopher, Larry . . .?"

16

"You know, I had a good friend named Earl. What do you think?" he asks.

"That sounds great," I say, "and I'll be Grace, but not as scatter-brained as in George Burns and Gracie Allen. And I'll change the children's names, too."

"So it will be Earl and Grace. I like it. And Gracie will be telling all the stories based on our lives."

"Yes. And every aspect of our lives. Because in life there are funny parts, serious parts and sad parts. I want to cover all of them."

"Good idea, Annie. To keep the readers interested."

"Yes. And I'd write about Muskoka, of course."

"You could even try writing for that small weekly newspaper that we get at the cottage, for starters."

"That's a great little newspaper. I love all the articles in it. Do you really think I could write well enough?"

"Yes, I do. Why not start with the tale you're about to tell me about the card table," he suggests.

Part 1

Rose-coloured tea:
Tales from yesteryear

Not just any card table

A regular old card table – why was it so special? Its surface was a pretty lime green, make out of some kind of fiberboard looking like a square of tightly woven linen coated with clear varnish. Its metal border was brown, the colour of an Aero chocolate bar. The four legs, although a bit scratched, were as strong that day in the new millennium as they'd been when her parents had first used it for bridge games in the thirties, or thereabouts.

Grace's mother would sit at it every year at Christmas time in front of the living room fireplace, accompanied by the sound of crackling and spitting logs. Before bedtime her mum would call Grace to come and sit at the little table with her. Already on the table lay pencils, a lined writing pad and an eraser. Staring at the table's shiny surface, Grace was fascinated by the movement and changes of colour and light reflected by the flames in front of them.

How important she felt sitting in the living room, just she and her mum, no father or brothers bursting into the room to spoil the magic moment. This was her time with her mum, when she'd name all the things she hoped Santa would bring to her while her mum wrote with rapid pen strokes on her pad. There could be as many as twenty items on that list before her mother would suggest that Santa might not have enough room in his sack. "Goodness," she'd said once, "he might get stuck coming down the chimney!"

Grace stopped willingly at twenty but never forgot to ask her mum to read her list back to her in case she'd forgotten something. Once it was finalized her mother would fold it in half and have Grace place it at the edge of the fireplace where Santa would find it.

Could Christmas Eve possibly be cozier? How joyful she felt, wrapped in her cocoon of naiveté and innocence!

It was one of her favourite nights, but the hard part was waiting for Santa to slide down her chimney. After she'd been put to bed and kissed good-night, she'd creep out of her room and stalk along the hall to perch on the top stair and wait for a glimpse of Santa through the wide open living-room doorway. Not once did she spy him. She didn't dare stay long for fear of getting caught. Her parents had warned her that Santa comes with gifts for the good little children only after they have fallen asleep in their beds. Disappointed, Grace would creep back to her room and into bed. Despite lying on her back with both ears uncovered in order to listen for the sleigh landing on the roof, she'd always fallen asleep before the jolly, fat fellow's arrival.

Disaster struck one year. After folding the list, her mum left the room to speak on the telephone down the hall. Having picked up the list and placed it by the fire, Grace also left the room to go upstairs for the next part of the Christmas Eve ritual in their house. That was when it was her father's turn to share the anticipation of Christmas with his little girl by reading Clement C. Moore's *The Night Before Christmas* to her. Afterwards, he tucked her in bed, kissed her and called Mum to give Grace her good-night kiss.

Mum came in asking, "Grace, what happened to Santa's list? I can't find it anywhere."

"But I left it beside the fireplace, Mummy."

"It's not there." Grace, Mum, and Dad trudged back downstairs to look for the precious list. There at the edge of the fireplace smouldered a pile of feathery, grey-black ashes.

Pointing, Grace cried, "That's my list!" Tears poured down her pale cheeks.

What a hard time Dad and Mum had convincing her that Santa had already heard her dictating the list! Finally, in desperation her mother declared, "I remember everything on that list and I'll write it out again and leave it for Santa."

"But I can't remember everything I asked for!" Grace uttered between sobs.

Because her gentle mum felt that her daughter was grown-up enough to know the truth about Santa Claus and the tooth fairy and the Easter bunny, that turned out to be the last time Grace sat at the green card table to recite her list for Santa.

The card table goes to school

Even though she usually sat at the front of the classroom, as advised by the ear, nose and throat doctor, kindergarten was a nightmare for Grace. How she'd clung to the doctor's explanation: it was her crutch for many, many years. Following the meeting with the doctor, she'd convinced herself and explained to her friends that she was deaf.

Never mind that Dr. Wright had merely hinted at such a diagnosis saying to her mum, "Mrs. Beaverbrook, although I detect no scarring, she displays the same behaviour as a deaf person." Back then it certainly never occurred to her that if she had really been deaf she would not have heard what the doctor was telling her mother, for he'd turned his back to Grace and he'd spoken quietly in doubting tones precisely so that the troubled child would *not* hear! "If Grace sat up at the front she would, no doubt, pay more attention to the teacher's instructions."

At school, for example, when the kindergarten class was divided into table-setting groups in which each participant played the part of a utensil, she was always a spoon, sometimes a soup spoon, sometimes a dessert spoon, and once a coffee spoon. If she'd been a fork she'd have eventually gotten it right, for the fork always was the first to take his or her position and always lay down on the side of the table mat closest to him or her - the left side, in fact.

As an adult looking back, she recognized that the teacher had used this method to ensure that the whole table setting would start off on the right foot, so to speak. After all, the children were only four or five years old and not all of them knew their right from their left. Whenever it was Grace's turn to lie down beside or above the mat pretending to be some kind of spoon, she'd always flung herself beside the fork.

It was never fun and she'd felt like a failure.

Because her surname began with 'B' and there were no children with surnames beginning with 'A', she was supposed to lead the class for its daily march into the assembly hall. The child behind her always held her bony shoulders to steer her in the right direction. Directions and sequences, such as Wednesday's coming after Tuesday, were too much of a challenge for poor Grace. Ballet classes and square dancing were impossible, too, but she never cared for the ballet anyway.

It wasn't until a generation later, when her younger son, Matt, started grade one and was diagnosed with a specific learning problem, that she discovered that she, too, had suffered from the lack of motor-audio-visual coordination. No wonder she had an inferiority complex! No wonder her parents decided to keep her home for grade one.

Grace also loved the green card table for its happy association with making the Santa Claus list with her mum and for its use at her parents' small parties, especially for noisy card games. From her bedroom upstairs Grace could hear the knock, knock of knuckles on the table accompanied by a victorious voice declaring "Knock, knock." Knock rummy was exciting; bridge was boring except when loud arguments broke out.

When her mum put up the table in the living room one morning in September, she explained that this was Grace's first day of grade one and Cousin Jane would be her teacher. What a great choice, for Grace adored her oldest cousin. This kind of grade one wasn't a bit like school except for the new supplies, the note pads, pencils, and much more. There were colouring books, picture books, a metronome, and cardboard charts that Jane had made, which had arrows pointing in different directions.

Sitting at the card table in her own house with her beloved cousin, sharing recess with her, playing with marbles and naming their colours, earning stars and doing arithmetic with real apples – this was fun! The mornings whizzed by.

Some of her friends were envious that she didn't have to go to school but they accepted the explanation her mother had given to her. Mum had said that Grace needed a year off because at school she'd caught too many colds.

Perhaps her naiveté was pathetic, but it did her more good than harm.

Grace discovers alcohol

The card table came in handy for a different kind of lessons, drinking lessons. For a couple of months every Friday when Grace came home from school, the little table would be set up with a shot glass, stir sticks, an array of different shaped and coloured bottles, decanters, a jar of olives, an ice bucket, and a pretty dish containing peanuts. Completing the scene would be bowls of chips and crackers spread with cream cheese or celery sticks stuffed with it. One time only (but never again since it ended up being a complete failure), a jar of anchovies awaited her testing.

Never ever did a bottle of ginger ale grace that table! She was informed that using 'mixes' spoiled the taste of the whisky, be it rye or scotch. On the day on which she was learning to drink rum, Coca-Cola made its appearance. Actually, she'd have preferred to drink the coke undiluted right then and there.

Grace had reached the sophisticated age at which she'd be invited to cocktail parties and her parents wanted her to be absolutely certain about her tastes and especially her limits. Each Friday a different drink was tried. Generally speaking she didn't much like any of the drinks but because it was her father's favourite, she'd settled on rye with water. Martinis, Old Fashions and Whisky Sours were dangerous. She'd found that out one Friday when the whisky sour didn't taste like it contained any alcohol at all and she'd consumed hers rapidly.

In fact, Grace was very inhibited about her body and one whisky sour was enough to oil her hips, brighten her cheeks, and put enough 'come hither' sparks in her dark eyes to send alluring messages to the opposite sex. Heck, she could even do the hula-hoop! Sherry was even worse and she fully understood why there were such things as tiny sherry glasses. The first simple sip would dive instantly into all her joints and give her a lovely, though debilitating, buzz.

As for the snacks, well, they were a treat (except for the anchovies) but no match for her after-school spoonfuls of peanut butter taken straight from the jar.

The first Friday that she came home to find the card table missing from the scene, she knew she had graduated. Her parents were proud of her and now expected her to stay out of trouble. Indeed, Grace never did become a big drinker.

Take me out to the ballgame

"Earl, you know how our parents used to say, 'Back in the good old days when we walked to school rain or shine instead of being chauffeured everywhere by our parents'?"

"Yes, I certainly do. I don't know how many times they reiterated that, but it was boring."

Grace loved Sundays. Now was her chance to settle in for a nostalgic discussion with her husband. She'd noticed that he'd abandoned his crossword puzzle and had a cold beer in his hand. Leaning back on the sofa she crossed her legs and picked up her knitting. Automatically Earl placed his hand on her knee.

"They were boring, that's for sure. And I remember how they'd look at each other and laugh and I'd fall into the trap every time and ask what the joke was. Mum would say, 'You think we're bragging? Wait'll I tell you what my parents used to tell me! They claimed that they rode to school rain or shine. On horseback'!" Chuckling, Grace continued, "And Mum told me that that made her jealous."

"I don't blame her. By the way, what are you leading up to with those little memories?" He asked giving her knee a gentle pat. "Or are you simply in one of your nostalgic moods? You'll have to excuse me, the Expos are on. Care to join me?"

"Maybe."

"You'll enjoy it, Gracie. I promise." Then he added: "You've no idea how entertaining Dave Van Horne can be. Or Joe Cannon, for that matter." Suddenly Earl bent over double, nearly rolling off the sofa.

"Earl! What's the matter? Are you sick?" She reached for his hands but he grabbed her face and tilted it upwards.

"Look at me, Grace, I'm laughing. I'm having one of my laughing fits. Let me catch my breath. Sorry, I didn't mean to frighten you. Ha, ha! Oh, I can't stop."

"It's okay, take your time. But please tell me what brought this on. Is it something I said?"

Finally he composed himself. "I'm remembering some of the funny things I've heard on the radio during Expos broadcasts. I forget who it was that said 'holo somers.'" He paused to regain control. "Oh, dear, don't ever say that listening to the ball game is boring. For one thing, if there isn't something going on in the field, there's certainly something happening in the broadcast booth at all times."

Suddenly Grace's expression changed from one of puzzlement to glee, "Oh, he meant solo homers. I get it. It's a bit like when an announcer is being trained and just before he goes on the air for his first live broadcast someone reminds him to open with 'This is the Canadian Broadcorping Castoration' and that's exactly what the fellow comes out with!"

"You actually heard that on the air?" Earl asked.

With a shrug she replied, "Nope, but my brother used to work for the CBC and he often told me funny stories like that."

"I can imagine. Okay, let me go on about baseball. Once I heard Ken Singleton complaining during his commentary about how one of the players was running the bases. He said, and I quote, 'He's nonchalanting it.' Isn't that something?"

"Yes, it is – sort of the same way you pick up your clothes, right, Earl?" She teased, poking his chest with her finger.

"And the way you disregard your budget when you go shopping without a list. In fact, I bet you leave your list behind on purpose."

She grinned impishly, "Well, I've certainly never been accused of being a perfectionist, dear husband."

"And I get the hint, dear. Anyway let me get us back into a laugh mode again, alright?" He rubbed his chin, "Oh, yes, once I heard coach Bobby Cox say, 'The Blue Jays have some get-evening to do.'"

"That's a good one."

"Oh, there's more," Earl continued. "This is my favourite. Partly because it was a Sunday afternoon double header and the poor announcers had to fill in a large space of time with baseball chatter, I guess. You know, while the pitcher is warming up and between the top and bottom half of each inning and during the seventh inning stretch."

"What's that? I forget."

"You know, that's when the fans stand up to stretch their legs between the two halves of the seventh inning."

"Of course, I remember," Grace nodded.

"And usually the music is blaring 'Take Me Out to the Ballgame' and the fans, many of them well fortified with beer, lustily join in. I'm telling you, Gracie, that's one of the many baseball customs I love."

"What, the beer or the singing?" She prodded him in his ribs.

Suddenly he burst out laughing and with his face turning red he pulled a paper table napkin out of his pocket and wiped the sweat off his forehead.

"Please, don't scare me again. What is it this time, Earl?"

"Oh, it just came into my mind. It's my all-time favourite example of the joys of listening to the Expos games."

"Tell me about it, dear."

"Glad to. Dave Van Horne and Joe had good chemistry, I swear. It can't have been easy for Van Horne, the expert, to work with Joe Cannon, the neophyte. Mind you, Joe Cannon is no dummy – far from it! Remember him with Melanie King on CJAD every weekday?"

Grace nodded. "They were the best, the very best. I was so sad when Melanie moved to Australia and their regular show ended. It must have been awful for Joe."

"But at least he got to fulfill his boyhood dream of becoming a baseball announcer, even if he wasn't the best at that."

"No, he wasn't, although he improved after getting a few games under his belt, don't you think? He was good at interviews, though, when he talked with a player one on one at the end of a game. Now and then I hear him doing sports stuff on the CBC." She sighed, "Such a pity."

"Why do you say that, dear?"

"Oh, it's just that it seems a real waste of his talent. He was an excellent radio journalist, so knowledgeable about world affairs, history and our politics. What I liked especially was his sense of humour: he always had Melanie laughing."

"By the way, Gracie, he hasn't lost his sense of humour. Now, let me finish telling you about the hilarious comments that came out of the mouths of Dave and Joe one Sunday afternoon. This is just from memory, mind you, and I'm probably leaving out some of the detail. To appreciate it you have to understand baseball so you'll get it, I think. Here goes:

"Dave said 'There's a pigeon behind the mound'."

"Joe said, 'He hasn't moved'."

"Dave said, 'He missed the sign'."

Grace cackled and Earl carried on. "Dave said, 'This is a multilingual city – the coach can talk to him in Pidgin English'."

More guffaws from Grace.

"Joe joined in saying something about the pitcher needing a good windshield and topped it off with, 'He can't wind up because he has to protect his head'."

Earl continued, "Apparently the pigeon moved and Dave said, 'The rules state that you can't have more than one runner on a base at a time, so as all the bases are full the poor pigeon doesn't have a safe base left to go to'."

Grace enjoyed a bout of hysterics of her own.

The dress

She was wearing a dark green wool dress that was obviously homemade, as it didn't hang quite right. The sleeves were puffed (perhaps a little too much), long and buttoned at the wrist with imitation brown leather buttons. The same buttons, only larger, decorated the front of the dress, double-breasted style. It was a fairly pretty and original dress, but it successfully covered up any femininity that might be budding underneath. A string of pearls glistened at the little V-neck.

Leaning against the mantelpiece, she watched the dancers. Her hands did not know where to go – should one rest on the hip while the other supported her chin, while her elbow perched on the mantelpiece? No, that just did not feel right. Down went both hands, straight against her sides pointing stiffly to the floor. Much better.

Aha, what's this? A tray of food appeared in front of her and, happily, each hand had a job to perform. The slender fingers of her right hand grasped a dainty sandwich. Careful! The chopped egg was squishing out while the other hand held an olive. She bit into the olive and a shudder caused her pearls to realign and sparkle. The sudden look of consternation on her face revealed her predicament: where to put the dashed olive stone? She'd hated the olive anyway, she'd only picked it up to give her hands something to do. All the other girls had a partner's hand in one hand and a padded shoulder underneath the other.

She'd found a solution at last. As no one was watching her, she popped it inside her dress at the 'V'. To her relief the music stopped and she could join her friends. En masse, they left the room and mounted the wide staircase to go to the powder room. Once there, they huddled in front of the small mirror reapplying lipstick. Grace (in the green dress) rubbed camphor ice over her drying lips then hastily put a dab of Revlon's 'Tangerine' on them. After having carefully smeared the lipstick on evenly with her fingertip, she rubbed the same finger on her cheekbones. So that was where her healthy colour came from! Strains of 'In the Mood' drifted into the little room and the group emerged, giggling again, to dance once more. Surely this time the wallflower would get her wish. But she didn't.

Once seen as a wallflower, one would always be stuck with that painful role. She played it with pride, and a touch of hope. The hands started assuming various positions and the mantelpiece again became her backrest as she stood there watching.

What humiliation for her to spend the rest of the evening patronized by the hostess who was, of course, only trying to be kind to her sixteen-year-old guest, the daughter of her best friend. Eventually her son went and asked the unfortunate girl to dance as did one or two other youths, the ones with glasses and pimples.

This was Grace's first dance. The next one she attended was a 'formal'. For this first 'formal' she wore a daffodil yellow dress whose bodice was gathered like a Ripley bathing suit. The colour set off her black hair better than the green had. Dangling from her wrist was the program with twenty dances on it. Number 10 was known as the supper dance. The supper and the last dance were the important ones because usually it was the boy who would take you home who signed up for these.

Grace's program never got more than half filled at these private Toronto balls, most of which took place in Rosedale or Forest Hill. They had great live bands and Grace took to hanging around near the band as though she knew some of the players. Between sets the orchestra members talked to her, not out of pity but because Grace knew a lot about music and the different Big Bands. Her older brother had taught her all this useful stuff, that Tommy Dorsey played the trombone, Harry James the trumpet and the names of their themes and greatest hits. Hence, she had something better to do than hold up the wall.

Wait a minute! How would she get her supper if she didn't have a partner to gallantly fetch it for her? There were times she simply went without supper altogether and sat with a few couples to avoid the degradation of having to go alone to the big table and load up a plate and pick up the punch. Sometimes her brother would have signed her program for the important supper dance. Other times sons of her parents' friends would sign up for a 'duty' dance, but rarely for the supper or last one.

Grace had an arrangement with her mother whereby if she didn't have a partner for the last dance she would call home and her mother would pick her up. The hosts and hostesses never guessed that Grace was leaving alone when she thanked them for the lovely time. She managed the escape unobtrusively, and no dancers took any notice of her departure.

Leaving those 'formals' was easy compared to leaving her beloved school of eleven years. After graduating with honours from her all-girl private school, she promptly did the obvious thing: applied for Pass Arts at Trinity College, University of Toronto.

That last summer before university she found the best place to put her hands, one around a lighter and the other gripping a cigarette. To learn to do this she'd gone through lessons, choking, tremendous laughter, and then finally victory – inhaling then vomiting for two whole days. It was worth it, though.

Too many girls from private schools had applied for entrance to Trinity College and Grace was one of the many who had to accept humiliation and go to an ordinary college. Funny thing though, by the time she'd learned of her rejection she'd already discovered enough of the outside world working as a waitress at The Glenmount Hotel on the Lake of Bays, and opted for University College anyway. And it was a good thing, too, because any trace of snobbishness she might have picked up at her private school soon disappeared at University College.

Popular as ever with the girls, she was rushed by lots of fraternities – that's what they called girls' sororities at U of T. She was pledged and finally initiated into the fraternity of her choice. That, however, was the initiation into another one of life's horrid growing up experiences for Grace, 'football weekends'.

Of course, she had to go on a football weekend, and why not McGill's since she was majoring in French. Somewhat short of funds, she packed her suitcase with last year's party dress to wear on the all-important Saturday night date after the game. She also took along her skirt with its five pleats in the middle of the back. These pleats, besides being in style, also gave her the appearance of having a sexy seat (private school girls didn't say 'bum') when in reality she was flat-bottomed. Anyway, the train trip to Montreal was a real adventure and she even got to play a few hands of bridge (one of the good things to come out of belonging to a fraternity) with a couple of members of the football team.

By halftime at the stadium all the fraternity sisters with whom she had come had dates – all but Grace, whose only sin was her lack of self-confidence. Aware of her situation and without a date himself, as his fiancée hadn't been able to come for this weekend, the team captain did the right thing. He escorted her on the rounds of fraternity houses and hotel rooms where the hilarity got better and better and they ended up at a nightclub, the likes of which would never grace the streets of Toronto-the-Good! The jokes and shows got dirtier and dirtier and Grace more and more embarrassed. Her laughter was harsh and false, but her friends were prostrate with hysteria. They thought that they were just about as funny as the comedians and certainly more attractive.

The team captain delivered Grace to the door of her room at the Laurentian Hotel, no doubt heaving a sigh of relief at shedding the encumbrance and feeling in a big rush to get back to the wild parties.

Meanwhile she got more sleep that night than her fraternity sisters. She also developed a case of swollen eyes. Her Liberty dress lay forlornly on the back of the hotel chair and her skirt with the pleats never got out of the suitcase. Nor did she feel much like wearing her new sloppy joe sweater that she had bought from a friend who had gone to Buffalo to shop.

Sunday, when her 'sisters' went out for brunch with last night's dates or some McGill type who'd taken their fancy and vice versa, Grace admired the view of the park opposite her hotel window. Some girls were riding with boys in the back of calèches atop Mount Royal, while she was racking her brain to think of someone she might know in Montreal to telephone.

The train ride home was pretty good for Grace. She fitted right in and played great bridge. Just about every member of the team wanted her as bridge partner and she shared cokes and sandwiches with them. She was exceedingly cheerful but secretly couldn't wait to get home.

It's called putting on a good face and Grace would have much preferred to put on a good, sexy, expensive dress and lure all the fellows like her fraternity sisters did so easily. But university was expensive, all those books, too, and fraternity fees were a virtual extravagance. She had been lucky her parents had been able to give her the money for the train tickets and hotel room. She knew it was hard for them.

When she walked in the door back at home the look on her face prompted her mother to say instantly, "Tomorrow we're going out to buy you a new dress." How did she know?

Off they charged Monday afternoon, mother and daughter, to choose The Dress. Boutique after boutique dressing rooms were left devastated, saleslady after saleslady nonplussed and with most harassed looks on the departure of the two determined females.

Well, old reliable Simpson's proved to have just what they were looking for, even though they hadn't really known, themselves.

The dress had a V front and back, the back's V more rounded and lower than the front's. It came in very tight at the waist, showing off her flat tummy, and flared at the top of the hips to give shape and rhythm which didn't really exist in Grace's still somewhat school-girl figure.

The material was the absolute *pièce de résistance*: shot taffeta. Black one moment, now midnight blue, then indigo. It played tricks on you and the dark colours gave her a 'woman of the world' look. It shone with an eye-catching flash. As for the sound it made, swish, shhh . . . divine! It zipped up on the side and this time not a button in sight. Oh, yes, it also had a kind of ruffle you could stand up or lie down along the neckline and over the shoulders.

She tried it on that night to show it off to her father. The dress passed muster except that her bra showed at the back and she knew she'd have to wear the dress without one. A strapless bra wouldn't do as she didn't have enough to fill one. When shedding the pretty party dress she decided to see how it would look minus the bra.

Her mother had a different idea, however, insisting that Grace give it to her to take in the back a little.

"You'd think they could at least sell us a dress with the zipper on the right side," she remarked. "We paid enough for it. Still, it is a beautiful dress, and I have to admit you look radiant in it, Gracie."

"The zipper is on the right side, Mum."

"That's the wrong side."

"You're right! I knew something felt funny when I was doing it up. But what's wrong with the back? I love it."

"I do, too, dear, but it needs a tuck or two over your shoulder blades."

"Wait a minute, do you suppose?" With that Grace pulled the dress back on, zipped it up, and burst out laughing. "How about that? Does the back look better? Wow, is the front low!"

"My goodness, we bought it backwards. Grace, what will your father say when he sees it now?"

"Can you tell I'm not wearing a bra?"

"Jump up and down a bit." She cast a critical eye over the scene, detected no movement, and responded still laughing, "Well, it's a snug fit so nothing bounces but it certainly is low. I mean you can see your cleavage."

"What cleavage?"

"Oh, don't you worry, the signs are definitely there to tease onlookers."

"Mum!" Grace saw that her mother could not control her mirth. "I'm keeping it, Mum. You don't even have to do any alterations. I don't need a bra and it's perfect."

She wore the cleavage dress to a small cocktail party given for her best friend who was getting married in six months. It was her first engagement party and how she would have loved to be in her friend's situation! Nevertheless, boys flocked around Grace, found her conversation scintillating, her jokes excruciatingly funny and her company most desirable. Not one, not two, but actually *three* of them asked her out for a date after the party. They weren't hesitant, either, to compliment her on her dress.

The dress certainly did its bit. She felt so good in it she couldn't resist a comeback with each compliment, "It's my cleavage dress. If I hadn't tried it on backwards my parents would never have bought it."

Of course they knew she was joking. She was a card, that Grace, and so attractive. They wondered why they hadn't noticed before.

The strained smile, awkward hands, hopeful look, and too loud laugh all went away with the arrival of the cleavage dress.

The card table moves to Grace's married quarters

By the time she had three children, Grace had to find a way to earn extra cash to pay for some of her extravagances without reporting just what they were to her husband. Because she had a bad habit of letting bills run up for the milkman and bread man and at the pharmacy, for example, she dearly wanted to pay them off. She was over the budget every month and knew that she'd have to catch up in a hurry before anyone found out. If she had her own money she *would* budget properly and no one would be the wiser about her sloppy habits.

Promising Earl that her earnings couldn't possibly put him into a different income tax bracket, she became a substitute teacher armed only with a Bachelor of Arts degree. During the 1960s teachers were in short supply and subs didn't require teaching qualifications, although they certainly were expected to teach all the subject matter listed by the teacher in her day book and to do all the marking thereof. It took a lot of nerve for Grace to apply, but as she limited herself to grades one to four she felt she could handle it.

Out came the green table again! This time Grace used it for practising cursive writing. Why hadn't she been taught it in her private school? What a nuisance! Unable to master g's, j's, k's, q's, r's, s's and z's in spite of spending hours at the little table and even with help from her oldest daughter, she had to find a solution. On the days when she was teaching the younger grades she'd get to school early and persuade the teacher next door to write out the letter of the day on the blackboard for her, plus the other penmanship exercises.

She decided that it was a great way to get to know some of the teachers anyway.

As it was such fun having extra spending money she also marked High School English compositions. That was a stretch! The papers arrived in batches of thirty to thirty-two about twice a month. Sometimes those papers rested on the card table placed so well out of the way that she found she could ignore them quite successfully for weeks at a time.

Once she sat down to mark them, however, it became hard to pry her away from them. They were far more interesting than library books. She corrected the papers accompanied by her trusty *The Canadian Oxford Dictionary* and M.H. Scargill's *An English Handbook*.

Finding the time taken away from her interaction with the children and watching hockey games on television, she gave up that job after six months. From then on, the card table became a card table again for games such as Rummy, Cheat, Go Fish, Hearts, and especially Bridge.

No ordinary mother

A saint. That was my mum. She was loving yet undemonstrative, fair minded, thoughtful, gentle, sweet, fun and funny, and unselfish. When she died many people told me she was the finest person they'd ever known. They were right.

Every night she went down on her knees beside her bed to say her prayers. Yes, she went to church once in a while but never preached. She wasn't puritanical – heaven forbid! The way she lived her life, the wonderful way she related to people of all ages and walks of life, made her special. I always knew this and truly tried to be like her.

Even though she was a product – or perhaps victim – of Victorian Toronto, she was not a prude, although she inadvertently led me to believe that as a teenager not only should I not *show* my feelings, in public especially, but also I should not *have* feelings. Believe me, such a mistaken grasp of my mother's attitude often had me wondering why I was so different from everyone else, for indeed I had feelings, all kinds: worship, longing, jealousy, anger, guilt, and pride, for example. All my friends appeared to coast through adolescence peacefully. Of course I was envious!

Thinking back about my genuinely saintly, beloved mother, I remember always being happy because she was my mum. To tell the truth, because of her I was the envy of all my friends. I was lucky and I knew it. I mean how many of my friends could boast about having a duck hunter for a mother? Boy, was she a good shot! Also, she was better at fly-fishing than anyone, male or female, old or young. My children adored fly-fishing for speckled trout with her.

She wasn't perfect, you see, and therefore she was interesting. Heck, she swore, but not with vulgar or sacrilegious expressions. 'Darn' was her strongest expletive. She smoked sometimes. When she was expecting guests at home she was impossible, not herself at all. Well, guess what, I'm just the same!

Her closet was always in such a mess that I used to happily reorganize her clothes, putting them on hangers properly so that they wouldn't crease or show blisters where a hanger's point had played its havoc. Sometimes I've wondered if she even noticed my meddling. Her disorganized clothes-hanging habit never changed and I certainly didn't receive any recognition for keeping her in better shape. Actually I'm glad she didn't thank me, because touching her clothes and admiring them was simply an act of love.

Although she dressed smartly and always looked pretty, she was unaware of it: she was incapable of showing off. Her only display of vanity pertained to her dainty, little feet.

Able to laugh at herself, Mum certainly had me laughing when she started to talk about "Naked" Cohen when we were discussing a play we'd gone to at Niagara on the Lake. What kind of Freudian slip was that!

Even when she was in her early eighties Mum wasn't averse to getting down on the floor to play with the dog, crawling around on her hands and knees, stopping, starting, chasing, making silly noises, and acting quite the antithesis of her dignified self. She made me proud.

Not once did I hear my mother and father have an argument, but I knew they had some doozies a few times. One afternoon while stepping off my school bus, I saw my father, a large bouquet of flowers in his hand, hovering on our front steps. How relieved he looked when he saw me approach! With a sheepish grin he urged me to go in ahead of him. There were other times when a vase of store-bought flowers graced the top of the upright piano. Since my father ignored birthdays and anniversaries, those flowers were a huge apology, no doubt about it.

His adoration of my mum was never in doubt, although he was unsentimental and hated displays of affection. For our upbringing it was Mum who nurtured my two brothers and me. Apparently, after he first saw me, born at seven months weighing four pounds, my dad told everyone that I had a good golf stance.

No wonder I grew up with a distorted sense of self! Certainly there was plenty of fun in my household and my parents' sense of humour was splendid, contagious and very Canadian.

Although the excesses of my Victorian upbringing stem from Toronto-the-Good's influence, during prohibition no less, some blame must also go to some relatives, the inhibited souls who acted more British than the British. Of course it was natural that eventually my older brother and I would rebel and become more humanized, losing our stiff upper lips.

Being broadminded, my mother understood.

Some important things
I learned from my mother

Probably the most important thing I've always known is that happiness cannot be bought. I learned that from my parents' example and our simple lifestyle. Actually, I would have liked my parents to buy me a sailboat and figure skating lessons but I didn't have to be told that some of my wishes were outrageous. I mean, I didn't live by the water and belonging to the Toronto Yacht Club would have embarrassed and cowed me anyway. By George, being denied many of my yearnings made me what I am today, a dreamer who loves to write. Honestly, I still don't need much in the way of material things as long as I have food and shelter, pen, paper, and books.

My mother told me that if a job is worth doing at all it is worth doing well. Makes sense. She also quoted that old adage, "A stitch in time saves nine". She was right about that, too, and I tried to instil the idea into my children's heads, even though I wasn't a very good example. From her I learned how to hold my white gloves when out in public, how to use a knife and fork properly, that you start your potatoes in cold water when cooking them, and to always puff up the sofa cushions before going to bed. I would say that her greatest lesson for my safety was to look up and down the street before crossing and I did just that by looking up at the sky then down at my feet. Fortunately Mum witnessed my mistake and gave me a demonstration. Writing a bread and butter letter after staying overnight at someone's house is inbred in me as well as thanking people for their gifts.

'Do to others as you would have them do unto you' was a cardinal rule in my house. It still is, of course. My mother's sense of fairness certainly rubbed off on me. Of great importance, she taught me not to *show* my feelings, period. I thought it was wrong to *have* feelings, an impression that has been difficult to overcome, unfortunately.

I'll always be grateful to her, for I know that life is what you make it and that material possessions are just the packaging.

Mercies and blessings

Be thankful for small mercies. How annoyed I'd get when someone threw that old adage in my face.

"Like what?" I'd ask. "You mean like getting a flat tire but having it happen when I'm driving practically in front of a service station?" Yes, that did happen to me more than once, and I was grateful, I guess. I was also told that I always landed on my feet, another goodie. This has always been true, but being reminded of this stroke of luck succeeded in wiping out any possible chance of my taking credit and thus failed to enhance my self esteem – silly me!

Winning a prize at a dance, even if it was a grease job and oil change, should have been reward enough for me – the gal who never won anything. At least that is how I felt when I was a little kid with an undiagnosed learning problem. As the only girl in my family, and the youngest to boot, my two brothers were allowed to do a lot of things I wasn't. You know, I'd be told,

"It isn't ladylike, Grace."

"So what!" I'd react.

I was horrified, for example, when my mother had to tell me, a growing eleven-year-old tomboy, "You cannot go around wearing boy's swimming trunks in public anymore." In public? Heck, I was somewhere outdoors on our one-hundred-acre country property playing with my brothers and their friends, for Pete's sake! Besides, I was hot.

I retorted, "I know. It isn't ladylike."

My mother's reaction really surprised me that time, "No, it's because you're looking too ladylike!"

"Oh," was my puzzled reply. I was no more ready for that life-changing prospect than I had been when my mum told me about Santa Claus. And, boy, did she lay it on! I mean she then added that she was the tooth fairy and those scrumptious chocolate rabbits and chicks and eggs I found hidden in strange places on Easter Sunday came from the store. Jeepers, next she'd be telling me where babies came from, but I was not ready for that, not at all. Mind you, I did have some sophisticated friends who had older sisters who tried to tell me a few unwelcome, and probably distorted, facts of life.

I do confess that unlike my brothers, it was okay for me to cry over things like scraped knees, spilt milk, sad songs, and movies. I loved a tearjerker! Bette Davis in 'Now Voyager', Kate Hepburn in 'Summertime', Ingrid Bergman in 'Casablanca' and

Simone Signoret (my favourite actress, although I was jealous of her because she was married to Yves Montand) in 'Ship of Fools' really opened my floodgates. Barbra Streisand did the same thing to one of my daughters, who shall remain nameless, in 'The Way We Were'. Did her brothers, not Barbra's, ever tease her!

My background was studded with warnings – in my house there lived a sort of mother's helper, a Bible student, who tried to teach me to carry a knitting needle on me whenever I travelled in the streetcar in case strange men got too close to me. Despite her tut-tuts, smacking lips and rolling eyes, I failed to develop the sort of fear of men that she had.

No one had to tell me to count my blessings, for mine were many. I grew up in a loving family that enjoyed singing together while doing the dishes, laughing, reading, and spending summers and weekends in the country either in Muskoka or the rolling hills of Mono. A love of nature is second nature to me, and yet I grew up also exposed to city life and city lights. Yes, I knew the best of both worlds. Also, having two big brothers made me learn to succeed in sports at an early age. I skied, skated, sailed and swam. They played hockey and football; I played field hockey, basketball and ping pong.

Today, happiness is the arrival of autumn. I find myself looking forward to cooking and eating all the colourful produce available at outdoor markets. Quebec strawberries and corn were really good but I'll always be loyal to Ontario peaches. You cannot beat them! While in Muskoka we feasted upon the peaches, wild blueberries, field tomatoes, and Peacock corn.

After a spring and summer of wearing the same clothes over and over again, especially as I travelled abroad and at my husband's 'request' travelled light, I'm ready to put the tried and true summer wear away till next year. When I open the old trunk to dig out my fall clothes I always get super surprises. There I'll discover the odd top and pair of pants I'd forgotten I ever owned, making me feel as excited as I do in a bookshop.

Now here is a blessing you Muskokans can count on: the distinct changes of season four times a year. When fall begins, I adore it. The same goes for winter (my favourite), spring and summer. Saying goodbye to one season and hello to the next one is painless and adds spice to life. Each season introduces something new: chores, clothes, habits, outdoor activities, pumpkin pie, smells, and sounds. Did you see or hear any flocks of geese heading south? I am picturing Martha the mallard leaving Lily Bay and I wonder where she and other Muskoka mallards go.

What actually put me into the mood to write about small mercies was the sight of a new weed stretching its tentacles out on my lawn. Never, never could I resist a weed! How rewarding it is to gently but firmly pull one upwards and feel its root finally releasing its grip on the soil underneath. My favourite weeds to yank are the creeping ground cover varieties, because when you pull you get that tiny snap over and over as the roots escape, all from one horizontal pull. Lovely!

Heaven help me if there is clover cropping up somewhere where it doesn't belong, pretty though it is. Clover has to be plucked one by one and, more important, its leaves counted. That's my rule, no 'ifs', 'ands' or 'buts', and I am incapable of skirting around it even if it is a waste of time. One day I will find a four-leaf clover. Then, what else will I have to look forward to that most likely will never transpire?

I am not thinking about getting struck by lightning or hit by a bus.

Okay, I concede that raking leaves can be a tedious autumn chore if you let it. The trick is to rake every day, even if you don't get the satisfaction you get from accumulating a huge pile of leaves at the end of a single workout. I must admit that because of regulations enacted to protect our fragile environment, I cannot enjoy the sight, sound, and smell of burning leaves like we used to. Of course it is harder bagging leaves than burning them! Oh, well.

For many, Thanksgiving weekend constitutes closing up the cottage and saying goodbye to the lake, summer friends, swimming and boating, bonfires and roasting marshmallows and playing board games with family and guests because there is no television or computer up there.

Small mercy if you live on an island as we did, at least you can be thankful that you'll no longer have to worry about either the weather or whether the boat will start or if you have enough gas for those trips to the mainland to dump garbage or pick up guests. We often resorted to freezing our garbage to tide us over until we absolutely had to go across the lake anyway. We were adept at labelling. It never seemed worthwhile to cross just to get rid of stuff, although I realize the alternative was not that attractive. When we moved back to the city, taking out the garbage was a simple pleasure.

Each time I return to the city after my happy summer in Muskoka, I adore the way the crickets welcome me with their persistent, cheerful chirping. To me that is a city sound, one that staves off sadness.

Celebrating Thanksgiving serves as a reminder of many good things and I do thank my lucky stars and say thanks for the memories. Are you listening, Mr. Hope? So when you celebrate Thanksgiving, hopefully surrounded by family, be grateful for small mercies: that the stove works, that at last new episodes of your favourite shows are appearing on television, that the sun is shining, the leaves are falling. And that tomorrow will come.

If a tree falls

If it hadn't been for my dreaming of the cottage in Muskoka I don't know how I would have been able to survive the great ice storm of 1998 that settled upon us in Pierrefonds and elsewhere during the night of January 5th. Our power went off at 6:30 am, January 6th, and stayed off until 9 pm, January 13th. Too bad that when we'd gone to bed Monday night we'd turned the heat down to 15 degrees as we always do.

At the beginning I kept saying to myself, heck, we didn't have electricity at the cottage for our first three years there. We lit the cottage by kerosene and Coleman lamps and cooked on a propane stove, used coolers with bought ice to store food in. I'd remind myself it was truly romantic without hydro. I'd remember, in addition, that for three years we didn't have water except what we hauled manually from the lake. Nor did we have the convenience of taps, sinks with drains or a flush toilet.

Here I was stuck in Pierrefonds, Quebec, freezing and yet I could still turn on the tap and get cold water – we ran out of hot on the first day – and we were still able to flush the toilet. This was luxury compared to our first years on Lake Rosseau. Did I say 'luxury'? The temperature dropped to plus 2 degrees in the basement and below freezing upstairs in our bedroom. For four nights we slept fully dressed from head to toe, snuggled very close together under seven layers of covers which included a Hudson's Bay Blanket, comforters and sleeping bags.

While shivering constantly I would imagine summer days at the cottage where I'd be warm in bed listening to boats on the lake, loons – if I were lucky – and perhaps the odd mosquito. Jeepers, I could be getting a polka dot tan while sitting on the dock in a deck chair with an old parasol clamped to it. The parasol has succumbed to marauding Muskoka mice, who have munched much of its surface! Jumping jellyfish, what wouldn't I give for all of the above now? I'd give up my house in Pierrefonds, and, if I had the power (not hydro) I'd give up winter.

This last statement was entertained on the third morning when we were out of firewood, fondue fuel and we were running low on candles. We were contemplating which books to donate to the living-room fireplace, our only source of heat. We also contemplated old book shelves, wooden spoons (probably germ-ridden as I've had them since we got married forty-five and a half years ago), picture frames in need of repair, hockey sticks, and even a pair of ancient cross country skis.

Normally, I adore winter.

Did I ever think of the sound of Muskoka mosquitoes, which drives me crazy? What about constantly dripping taps that we have turned on throughout the house to discourage our pipes from freezing?

On our fourth night of the deep freeze we were suddenly awakened by bad guys either stealing the silver from our attic or landing on the roof with ominous thuds, sliding on it and even sweeping it! It took me a moment to realize that I was not in Muskoka listening to squirrels on the roof or pine cones falling. It was, of course, tree branches losing some of their huge ice chunks and frozen pine needles attached to small twigs looking like fingers falling onto the roof.

While the house temperature remained around the freezing point, the wind and a thaw was playing havoc outside. In some ways this was one of the scariest aspects of the ice storm, when ice fingers and slabs showered our streets, cars and citizens. It then became unsafe to venture outside. You could not walk on the uneven frozen lumps that covered the ground completely and you were a target if you approached buildings or trees. This thaw did indeed remove much ice from the trees and wires, but certainly not the thickest deposits and especially not those piled on building ledges, billboards, overhead street signs, and lights.

It was these very ice fingers that we gathered by crawling on the solid ice that was our front yard, and then threw into our freezer to maintain freezing temperatures inside it.

However, after eight and a half days all the ice in the freezer had melted and most of our post Christmas turkey, quiches, stuffing, gravy, canapés, vegetables, seafood, and fish had to be thrown out. Now, even in mid-February, I'm not confident enough to buy ice cream.

True, our freezer let us down, but our telephone never did and our daily newspaper, delivered on time every day, kept us in touch with the outside world. Family and friends from Toronto, Bracebridge, Atlanta, North Carolina, New Hampshire, Paris, and London telephoned to enquire about our welfare. We were very touched, even though getting calls in the evening after we'd snuggled into our bed meant exposing fingers to a veritable icicle in the shape of a telephone.

On the fifth day our daughter Jessie in Pointe-Claire got her power back, but before we could move out we had to – guess what? – drain all the pipes, after driving from store to store to find plumbing antifreeze. Our experience with this task at the cottage made it feel routine and we ended up assisting many of our neighbours, who had never contemplated doing such a thing.

The worst ice storm of the century rates high on my list of scary phenomena. I've seen the swath of devastation that a tornado left in Port Sandfield. I've heard mighty thunderstorms and watched near hurricane-force winds churn Lake Rosseau. I've suffered from the ugly destruction caused by the caterpillar plague which invaded Muskoka a few springs ago, making the woods an unbelievable nightmare scene of dangling, thick caterpillar webs. I've been in a real pea-souper fog in London, England. I've experienced droughts in Muskoka and elsewhere in Ontario. I've even canoed on one of the main streets in Pierrefonds after heavy flooding.

Indeed, there is a sound that will haunt me the rest of my life, one that is terrifying as it builds up to a crescendo. It is a dry, crackling noise that suddenly ends in a great crash as a tree branch snaps from the unbearable weight of ice and falls to the ground, destroying wires, roofs, and cars and scattering ice in its wake.

Don't ask me if a tree falls in the forest and there's nobody there to hear it, does it make a sound?

Part 2

Woodland Tea:
Muskoka

Simply the lake

I've been trying to analyse what it is about being at the cottage that I love so much. So many events, so many memories.

My love of Muskoka began the first time I was up here, at Norway Point, when I was a baby. Even when my parents bought a one-hundred-acre piece of land featuring rolling hills, fields, cedar bush, a swift and full trout stream, an apple orchard, live elm trees, and an old wooden two-storey farm-house in the rolling hills of Mono Township, my loyalty towards Muskoka never wavered.

It was there at 'The Farm', however, that I enjoyed the taste of our own apples, be they 'Wealthies', 'Northern Spies' or 'Snows', as well as 'Katadin' potatoes. It was there that I learned to ride horses and to fly cast for trout. And, boy, did I ever love Rosemont's general country store, where my husband bought his first pair of jeans many years later! Doing the laundry at the laundromat in Alliston was just the same as doing it in Port Carling fifteen years later.

One Friday in 1981 Earl, Sarah, Jessie, and I drove to Muskoka to meet a real estate agent who had lined up some properties for us to look at on Lake Rosseau. As soon as we arrived at my cousins' at Norway Point after our seven-hour drive from Pierrefonds, we climbed into the agent's boat and proceeded to visit about six places. Not one truly tickled our fancy and we were a discouraged troupe eating dinner that night. The next morning my cousin said she would take us to a property nearby that was not listed with an agent and which, she feared, we might consider too treacherous, too high up from the lake.

It was love at first sight.

We came to an agreement with its owner, Mary, while standing in the woods overlooking Lily Bay. We shook hands to seal the deal – that's all it took. Mary told us that she often trudged through 'our' woods in the wintertime, hence Earl's decision to leave a chair on the veranda every winter for her to rest on.

Crazy though it sounds, my husband drove to and from Muskoka in one day in order to sign the final papers with Four Seasons Log Homes and with Larry English for the construction of our beloved cottage. He drove fourteen hours for a forty five-minute meeting!

The next summer, after sitting at a picnic table on Larry English's barge surrounded by beds, dressers, pots and pans, tables and mattresses, we arrived at 'Shonan' (the cottage) for our first night. That same evening we were awed by the sight of the full moon rising directly opposite us across the bay above a skyline of evergreens. It was a good omen.

My stays at the cottage have been happy and varied. One was the 'summer of Garfield', when I was alone up there with my comics-loving grandson, Lon. For three weeks he regaled me, non-stop, with tales of Garfield's antics. In no time I mastered the technique of nodding, frowning, laughing, and exclaiming at precisely the right moment without actually listening to Lon or ever looking at the silly cartoon character.

The following summer Lon, nearly nine years old, had matured greatly and we had fantastic discussions about the moon and the stars, World War II, Pierre Trudeau, democracy, materialism, freedom, apartheid, honesty, good versus evil, and so on. Believe me, I was certainly not bored by these conversations: I was astounded at Lon's knowledge and grasp of things.

Before we had our telephone, how many hours we spent looking through binoculars towards the church on the mainland for the arrival of a family member or guests waiting to be fetched in *Blue Champagne* (our first boat). For our first few years our children would pitch a tent on the church property if they arrived after dark and we would pick them up the next morning.

Every year we look forward to the first sighting of a merganser family whose presence we notice because of the bossy parent or aunt keeping the ducklings in line with much quacking. We are especially delighted when we spot a laggard suddenly racing to get to the front of the line, then sliding on to Mum's back for a free ride.

Such fond memories do I have of summers with Scrappy, Matt's Boxer, managing to fold a Frisbee in half with the help of her paw, mouth and the ground, then placing it in her mouth in order to carry it around like a security blanket wherever she went. When she needed to go into the woods to go the bathroom, she deposited it safely on the path beforehand, then picked it up again. That wonderful dog loved having swimming lessons conducted by Sarah (a life guard) in Sandy Bay and making up her own games such as running then jumping onto the Frisbee and sliding on it down the hill over and over again, like a child on a saucer in the snow. One time when Scrappy misplaced her Frisbee for a couple of days, she was despondent. Sarah and I were also desperate until we found it propped up against a tree by a path where she must have left it for one of her forays further into the forest.

We've had some great Thanksgiving weekends at the cottage. No wonder people come on organized bus tours to see the fall colours in Muskoka! With sons Jack and Matt as guides, we usually take two to three hours to walk through the woods to the southern tip of the island. Especially precious are the table centrepiece and place settings which Sarah's friend Sandy, knowing this would be her last Thanksgiving, created out of fungi, leaves, twigs, and mosses she collected during our walk.

In Bracebridge, our daughter Liv gave birth to her first child, Cole, while I waited all alone by the phone feeling helpless, nervous and in great suspense. However, I was certainly wishing that I was not stuck on an island this night of all nights.

Earl and I will never forget all those nights when we pretended to each other that we were asleep while we strained our ears to hear Jessie (aged fifteen, sixteen and so on) returning in the *Crestliner* at curfew time. Do I love the sound of that boat slowly rounding Whaleback and creeping along, then, turning gently into the slip! That's the one time that I actually appreciated the sound of our squeaky front door – ah, Jessie safe at home.

It's embarrassing. I'm frequently caught in that conversation of my generation about jet skis, the one where they complain about the noise, speed, audacity, you-name-it of jet skiers. I cannot join in the conversation for secretly I'm wishing I had one of those machines. They must be so much fun, maybe better than Rollerblades, which I also admire and covet. If I had jet skis, I wouldn't be a nuisance. To tell the truth, no jet skier has disturbed me in our bay, on the contrary, they've kept their distance from our dock and maintained a friendly smile – of *joie de vivre*, no doubt – and jauntily given me, standing slack-jawed and jealous on my dock, a typical Muskoka wave. One time Jack nearly caused a polite skier to tumble when the poor fellow looked at him standing on the end of our dock. You see, Jack had covered himself completely with clay that he had gathered from English Bay, to help pass the time while Lon was having a swimming lesson there. He was quite a sight, my thirty-four year-old son, and the jet skier, having decided (I guess) that this glistening, grey figure was actually a statue, was startled when he heard Jack laugh.

When I'm not here I often catch myself picturing the splendid view I have from my cottage perched high up above the lake. Every single time I sit down at the table on the veranda for a meal, I find myself saying, "What a view!"

Indeed, I realize that what I love most is simply the lake.

Blue Champagne:
a love story

She was exactly what we wanted and our very first boat.

We used to compare her to my battered Volkswagen Beetle (the 'Volksie') of the 1970's. That was an unreliable, almost human car that was a cinch to park. She used very little gas, allowed me great viewing of the road and surroundings, and didn't mind a few potato chips and popcorn pieces decorating the back seat.

A big surprise awaited me when I went to pick up our new purchase. She had a clutch and a gear shift, contraptions I didn't know how to use. I was a real klutz when it came to the clutch. Once, while trying to teach me to drive, my mother had showed absolutely no sense of humour when she saw me cross my feet after ordering me to put my foot on the brake.

Well, it was pretty much the same when we bought that first motor boat for our yet-to-be-built summer residence. It was a necessity because our new property, in Ontario's Muskoka area, was on an island. She was a fifteen-year-old, fibreglass, 14½ foot Peterborough. As our son Jack went to Trent University in Peterborough, Earl and I felt this was a good omen. Lovingly, we named her *Blue Champagne*.

The people who sold her to us had used her for fishing in Lake St. Louis off Dorval. We'd seen for ourselves that the waters in Lake St. Louis sometimes got very rough. We felt assured she could easily handle Lake Rosseau's temper tantrums.

Neither my husband nor I had ever run a motor boat before, except for a brief stint by my husband when he sat in the stern holding a handle and controlling speed and direction with the handle and its parts.

Blue Champagne was quite different, though. She had a steering wheel, a choke, an ignition key, a horn, a windshield, two bench seats, lights, a battery, and a 40-horsepower Johnson outboard engine.

It didn't take us long to discover that she was not ideal for transporting elderly aunts, for she felt every bump and appeared unsafe in high seas, of which there are plenty in Lake Rosseau. We also realized that our lovely shoreline, situated at the entrance of a picturesque bay, was exposed to the prevailing South Westerlies and therefore almost never wave-free. This meant that docking was a huge challenge. In our ignorance when first viewing the property, we had imagined that our piece of shore was protected from heavy winds by the small peninsula, known as Whaleback, to the west of us. But that was only on a calm day.

As we didn't have a dock at first, we used to moor *Blue Champagne* against a fallen tree that lay securely at the water's edge on a clear, sloping rock. This old tree, slippery and full of knobs, had holes, many of which we used to stand our tooth brushes in – hence the names Tooth Brush Log and Tooth Brush Rock.

Blue Champagne acquired its sporty look and feeling after I broke its windshield during an attempt to leap on to Tooth Brush Rock using the windshield for support. How we loved the wind blowing in our faces! We wouldn't let Earl replace it.

My enterprising husband did replace the horn, however, on the same day it stopped working. We used to tease him for saving old parts but we had nothing but praise for him when we listened to *Blue Champagne*'s new horn. He had added to her considerable charm by using our old Volksie's horn.

From time to time the steering wheel broke loose. As ours was such an old boat – some people dared to use the word 'wreck', what nerve! – we couldn't find the tiny part we needed anywhere. Not to worry, a coat hanger cut and twisted into a funny shape did the job. Some of our guests wondered why we insisted on keeping a coat hanger in *Blue Champagne* at all times. I explained that it was our spare tire and that confused them even more!

When the stern bench collapsed, we simply discarded it. *Blue Champagne* was thereafter twice as useful for transporting furniture, mattresses and lumber. Passengers had to sit on flotation cushions, life jackets or their own luggage – and once on our newly purchased pack-a-potty.

Getting *Blue Champagne* ready each spring required a weekend of work. First we had to remove the soggy mess of leaves and needles which had accumulated inside, then drag the boat off the beach into the cold lake, being careful not to tip up the bow too much and thereby thrust the propeller into the sand. Then, "Aye, aye, did anyone bring the transom plug?" We'd tow her over to our dock where Earl had the task of de-winterizing and spring cleaning the engine's parts and plugs and the lower unit. Last but not least came the sorting out of all the wires, squeezing them into tight places, and ensuring that the red bulb was put in the port side and the green on the starboard.

Have you ever had an Alzheimer's-like experience at night watching a moving boat that has its coloured lights reversed?

Some St. Jean Baptiste Day weekends (our Quebec June holiday), the black flies or rain interfered. While *Blue Champagne* was launched and ready for daytime use, the lights and horn had to wait a week or two for Earl to work on when he would return from Pierrefonds for his vacation. This usually presented no problem, because I, alone at the cottage, was certainly not about to go out on the lake at night; or so I thought!

But at 10:30 p.m. one night, Matt phoned me from Port Sandfield to announce that he and his friend would be arriving shortly at the church, our mainland pickup spot. Shiver my timbers, they weren't supposed to arrive until the next morning in daylight!

I knew how dangerous it was to go out on the lake in the dark without lights. Sure, it was easy for me to see boats racing all over the place – but they wouldn't see little me! I clamped the flashlight that has two lenses, one green and one red, on to the ledge where the windshield should have been, and taped two flashlights on to each side of the stern. Admittedly, they weren't easy for other boaters to spot because they kept slipping and pointing skyward. Next, I strapped a great big lantern that had a one-foot long neon light on to my back like a rucksack.

Lit up in style, I followed the shoreline from Lily Bay past Whaleback and over to Norway Point, then when I saw that there were no boats coming, dashed straight across the mile of open water to the church's dock. Wow, did she go!

Getting back to the island was safer, I felt, because the two passengers held the lights. The one in the stern held two flashlights, one in each hand with his arms outstretched, and my son kept the neon light aloft in the bow.

Once when Earl was leaving Wallace Marine he heard a sharp C-R-A-C-K in the bottom of *Blue Champagne*. He turned right around and had Irv Wallace put the boat up on the lift. Whew, no crack on the underside, but the one inside in the fibreglass stretched the full length of the hull. The old girl was cracking up and Irv told us he wasn't sure which would go first, the hull, or the engine – insulting! Such a tease, that Irv!

The split in the fibreglass was ugly but not dangerous. We patched it up and continued to use our beloved boat about three more years, always crossing our fingers when crossing the lake. She gave us yeoman service and didn't mind if a careless driver bumped her against a dock, or rock. That was part of her charm; she really never cared a hoot about her looks.

She did put her foot down, we soon found out, when it came to fishing. I mean, she simply refused to go on. You see, once she discovered the thrill of speed, there was no turning back, never! She may have felt she'd done her share of trolling in Lake St. Louis for her first owners. Now, she had tasted freedom in Muskoka.

You couldn't help admiring her spunk.

How did we discover this little eccentricity? She stalled without fail, anytime and anywhere when we moved the lever to slow or reverse – she had to think about it first. This bad behaviour made landing her fraught with difficulty: it took skill getting into position using a paddle. Thanks to her, I always felt that for docking I needed an empty dock and one that was long enough for Muskoka's famous paddle steamer, the Segwun, at least.

We were stymied finally when we could not find a way to either get the engine to start consistently (despite a new battery), or to get into reverse, or to keep her running long enough to get out of our bay. Sadly, we sold her to the brother of a neighbour and after tinkering with it for only one morning he roared out of the bay past our dock.

He was a genius with marine engines.

Blue Champagne, the ridiculous, has been replaced by *Pink Champagne*, the sublime, a 20½ foot Crestliner with inboard/outboard 200 horsepower motor and *Peewee*, a super little fibreglass (again!) punt with oars and/or a 2.2 engine.

Still missing you, *Blue Champagne*.

Skinny dipping

Let's face it, skinny dipping is a bit dangerous. But nothing adds more zest to an activity than a little fear. I love that challenge of placing my large towel in the best strategic position for rapid retrieval, undressing, if necessary, between boats crossing but not entering the mouth of our bay, then slipping into the lake.

Skinny dipping at night when you know you can't be seen and you can just float around stargazing without getting a sore back or neck, is particularly liberating. You might, however, encounter a bat or two swooping at objects in the moonlight. I've learned to stay out of the moon's path.

You may wonder why I bother to skinny dip at all, considering the risks involved? I'm telling you this: if the water is warm, it feels like velvet caressing you. If it's cool, its silken texture massages and stimulates every pore in your skin.

True confession: some of my best writing ideas are inspired by Lake Rosseau's caresses on my bare skin. Sometimes the inspiration becomes annoying, however, forcing me to get out of the water in search of a pencil and notebook before the 'brilliant' words escape me. Oh, well.

It's exhilarating how graceful one feels when swimming in the nude, with no encumbrances like slipping shoulder straps or bathing suit sections that fill with air. I truly feel like a porpoise and no one has dared deny me this self-portrait!

For night bathing you need to know your swimming spot like the back of your hand because you certainly don't want any surprises, like a sharp tree branch sticking up just high enough for your kicking foot to strike it and your reaction is that the stick is striking you! I've been known to startle my family with a piercing shriek all because my hand was 'grabbed' by a slimy rope dangling in the water behind our moored rowboat.

A friend of mine from Holland says that the highlight of her trip to Canada was moonlight skinny dipping in Lake Rosseau's seductive embrace. She had never had this opportunity in Holland. The North Sea wouldn't be very inviting. Nor would the beautiful canals, which branch out in all directions throughout this charming Lowland country, afford sufficient privacy.

One threat to my privacy, an unusual one, is my neighbour's seaplane. I mean, can he tell I have no clothes on from way up there above me, or should I tread water in a perfect perpendicular position? Jeepers, it's embarrassing when I detect his hand off the stick waving in a friendly manner. I'm most reluctant to wave back because I don't really want to encourage him and I also don't want to expose *any* parts of my body. Crikey, I wouldn't want him to crash! Maybe what I should do is kick frantically so that I'm shrouded in spray.

One romantic evening when Jessie's date had picked her up to look for a fun party on the mainland, Sarah and I nearly ruined our reputations and Jessie's summer, probably. Just as Jessie and her date were returning to 'Shonan' much too early, having given up on Port Carlings's social life, Sarah and I were scrambling to get out of the water to grab our clothes that rested slightly beyond our reach on a slippery, steep rocky spot beside the dock. The warning sound of the boat's motor had prompted us to make our graceful escape. M'gosh, his huge 6000 watt search light was illuminating the shoreline and heading straight for our white bodies!

Let me tell you, it is impossible to put on clothes over wet bodies, especially in a hurry. Our skinny dip had been a spur of the moment decision, hence no towels! Not to worry, with athletic prowess befitting Olympians we'd both managed to clothe ourselves, albeit minus any undergarments, and roll successfully into a convenient blueberry patch, where we lay flat and practically not breathing while Jessie leaped off the boat and waved goodbye to her date. Did we startle Jessie as she skipped past us while heading for the steps to the cottage?

Well, she deserved it.

Swimming in the buff at dawn, or soon thereafter, presents the usual challenges of boaters choosing our bay for fishing. One time I was already in the water enjoying my private swim when, lo and behold, a pair of males drifted quietly into the bay then proceeded to stand up in their runabout and drop in their fishing lines. They hadn't seen me and I stayed perfectly still while enduring their leisurely fishing expedition. Mind you, my legs got a fantastic workout that morning treading water. When the fishermen finally left I climbed out on to the dock feeling tired, hungry, waterlogged, and disgustingly wrinkled. On lazy Sundays if I've slept in a bit (as I'm wont to do), I have to rush to get in my swim ahead of the 'church parade' of boats en route from points south to attend Mass at St. John's Roman Catholic Church on the mainland, too close for comfort from our bay.

My treasured skinny dips do not take place at all in daylight when the family across the bay is in residence. This little problem, however, is being solved by the construction of a boathouse over our docks, thus allowing me to get in and out via one of the covered slips unobserved whenever I feel like it. This is really silly because I know my neighbours aren't remotely interested in my dangerous dips and, besides, they're inclined to sleep in anyway.

Will I enjoy it as much when I'm not faced with the fear of being spotted? You bet! There is absolutely no way you can replace that silky sensation produced by swimming in one's birthday suit.

Hooked

Hooked. I looked the word up in my dictionary and enjoyed discovering its many uses and meanings, origin and derivatives. A story needs a hook, for example. You can be hooked on the classics, or phonics. You (not I) can use a crochet hook, or hook a rug. You can hook up with a person, a funny way of putting it – I guess it means he\she got his\her hooks into you! Or you can have a hook-up, such as to a computer.

In Muskoka the most commonly used hook is, of course, the fishing hook.

Over the years Earl has acquired quite a bit of sophisticated fishing equipment to add to his substantial collection of tackle, tackle boxes and rods. He has, mounted on our 20 footer, both a downrigger and a fish and depth finder. When the latter is in operation you can forget your desire for peace and quiet. As you're moseying along, the darn thing beeps when the depth underneath you changes dramatically or a fish finds its way on to your screen.

Heck, that silly beep has even woken me up from my hammock-induced afternoon nap, coming from a fishing boat off the next point! Surely that's loud enough to scare away the fish. Jibing jellyfish! I was taught, not in a kindly manner, to shut up while angling. To me as a child that was by far the hardest rule of fishing. I used to wonder how people could say that it was *fun*. It certainly isn't fun when pointed, growing-ever-taller, jagged mountains darken your nasty depth finder screen. I mean, this is what's *underneath you* and, blimey, they can come out of nowhere in a real rush. That's when I shut off the machine and reverse. If I can remember how!

Regarding the downrigger, you'd better handle its appendage with the greatest of care. This is the ten pound-or-so black weight that pulls the fishing equipment downward. You don't want to drop it anywhere except, while attached, into the water. During its first trial run, Earl wasn't properly prepared and the ball (sinker?) and 200 foot cable became unattached when he was at a depth of about 150 feet. This is not like losing a little lure. No way would he get those essential parts back. Its weight alone would bury it instantly. Besides, it would be too slimy to handle, like a watermelon covered all over with Vaseline. Nor do you want to drop it unattached *anywhere*, especially on toes or toys.

Our first summer with the supposedly foolproof equipment all attached to the Crestliner cost us more in gas than we had spent any other summer. It would have been acceptable if the fish had taken an interest. They hadn't.

When our friends from Scotland came to spend a couple of weeks with us, my husband eagerly introduced Alan to fishing. For Earl, it was to be wonderful having someone to fish with, someone to either man the steering wheel or grab the net upon command, someone to relax with and enjoy the anticipation when you never know if or when you'll suddenly feel that tug on your line.

Within a minute Alan caught a fish and jerked it into the boat, but in the process the hook hooked his life jacket, which he was wearing. Earl suggested he not touch a thing because he was experienced with hooks and barbs and to wait till he dropped anchor and wound in his own line in order to come to Alan's assistance. By the time he turned to help him, three of the hooks on the lure had managed to become lodged where they shouldn't have been: one in the life jacket, one in his right index finger and one in his left thumb.

This was to be a big operation. Earl headed straight for our dock to get the car keys in order to drive Alan to the hospital in Bracebridge. The hook in Alan's thumb was stuck under the nail and Earl told Alan that he would probably need a local anaesthetic before having it removed, plus a tetanus shot. Before Earl had even landed the boat, brave Alan yanked the hooks out himself! Antiseptic plus good, clean Lake Rosseau took care of the rest, and the thumb recovered completely.

Not one to refuse a challenge, Alan went fishing with Earl again. I think he must have enjoyed it for he always caught keepers, but he let Earl do the unhooking thereafter. Earl kept telling Alan it was beginner's luck. The next year we stayed with our friends in Scotland. Their hospitality was superb. We ate 'smokies', haggis, oatmeal, and drank a lot more than a wee dram of whisky, of course. We also ate cod caught during Earl and Alan's first and only deep sea fishing expedition.

Guess who caught the cod?

The big one

If you're writing about Muskoka you cannot avoid fish tales. People think I'm exaggerating when I relate some such interesting events, but I don't have to because truth *is* stranger than fiction.

All her life, our youngest daughter has had an uncanny knack of catching fish no matter where she tries. Her friends will switch places with her, use her lures, her worms and her grasshoppers yet still it is only Jessie who catches the fish!

My mother was like that.

Jessie even managed to catch a small-mouth bass completely by accident while she slept through the night. She'd left her rod leaning two feet out of the rowboat with its hook about eleven inches above the water and had gone to bed. The next morning there was a pathetic-looking bass hanging above the water, no longer flipping.

A guest left his catch, properly killed, on the end of our dock while he went up the hill to the cottage to fetch a measuring tape or something. When he came back the fish was gone. We figured raccoons had found it.

Can you imagine his surprise the next morning when he found it again lying on the dock in the same place as the previous afternoon, very dead, but still whole. What he didn't know was that during my dawn dip I'd seen it lying on the lake bottom. This was one of those few days when the lake was like a mirror. By Jove, the slippery creature had been hard to retrieve! A net would have been nice.

One morning, fed up with spending money on gas and trying to do too many things at once in the Crestliner making all his fancy equipment (fish and depth finder plus downrigger) pay for itself, Earl went off in our 12½-foot rowboat with its 6-horsepower motor. He was actually just taking a quick turn around our bay and the next before breakfast.

Our guests and I found ourselves getting hungry and a bit worried. It wasn't like Earl to desert us like that, especially without his morning coffee.

Suddenly the little red boat hove into view rounding Laura Point. Humungous hollering (not an unusual occurrence) greeted us getting louder as Earl gunned the motor and steered towards the dock. Alarmed, all the guests and I raced down the cliff to the lake. We soon discovered that the thunderous shouting was both elation and pleas for help in getting his monstrous catch out of the boat. I thought he was exaggerating and being a bit silly.

This fish was so big it was *ugly*, reminding me of Charles Laughton playing 'The Hunchback of Notre Dame'. My husband had not been exaggerating one bit, and he had every right to brag.

What we saw lying in the bottom of the boat was a 17¼-pound 40-inch *whopper* of a Northern Pike. Having taken the prize to Irv and Richard Wallace to ascertain its species, we have pictures and witnesses to confirm this.

For Earl this was an *Old Man and the Sea* adventure. This was what he told us after he caught his breath. Tired of catching rock bass, he explained, he gave one last cast shoreward opposite Silver Craig. His lure became snagged, he thought, since it didn't come up to the surface like a normal fish would. Suddenly Earl saw a fish and guessed it was a lake trout. After playing it for about twenty minutes he managed to get it close enough to shove his net under it.

You should have seen his net with its aluminum handle bent almost double. At one point as Earl was lifting the fish, which was hanging face first three quarters out of the net over the gunwale, his glasses' cord became entangled with the net handle.

It is an instinct to safeguard one's glasses, especially when leaning over deep water. It must have been quite a problem for him, when he had to risk the loss of the biggest fish he'll ever catch in Lake Rosseau or the loss of his reading glasses, without which he wouldn't be able to clean the fish anyway.

Fortunately, the fish overcame his hesitation by flinging itself into the boat. We soon saw the reason for the cries for help. The monster was not truly dead and in one jerk could easily have hurled itself back into the lake. Our little bonker was certainly not designed for slaughtering such a spectacular, sizeable fish!

It took a concerted effort by Earl, Sarah, our burly guest (former police commissioner of Paris) and myself to get The Big One safely on to the dock.

Tracing him for our fish book was another challenge requiring four pages of computer paper. It took most of the morning for the two men to scale and clean the pike, then divide it up into portions for soup, that night's dinner and five meals (one for each of our children) plus future meals. It's a good thing we have a freezer.

Actually, in the end the eating of the prize was anticlimactic.

I never tire of listening to Earl describe, in most dramatic fashion, how he caught The Big One. It's a heck of a lot better than listening to his former frequent complaint, "There *are* no fish in Lake Rosseau!"

A fish out of water

Leaping lizards! What to do when out and alone in a rocking skiff with a live, genuine keeper flopping in the bow, my first small-mouth of the year? I mustn't lose him because he has to be traced and put in the family fish trophy book.

This book, I may say, is full of many great catches made by my son-in-law, one by my daughter's young friend, one by Earl, and that's it! You'd think that a family of seven and a couple of in-laws and a growing grandson would have a better record than that.

I mean this is our cottage. We live here all summer long. Well, I do, at least, since my husband works in the city (Montreal) to pay for it all.

My fishing problem was caused in part by the cost of boat gas and difficulty in getting it, since this backward boater has a hard time docking at gas pumps where I see moving boat traffic, a watching public and boats tied up everywhere. I had set out in the rowboat, with its 2.2 hp engine attached, bringing my rod, reel, lures, licence, life jacket, bailer, and my high spirits.

The 2.2 jauntily sputtered into its highest speed shoving the boat straight towards the rocky shore. Luckily the strong painters, still securely tied to the mooring rings on the dock – my mistake, but a good one – held the boat in position. After untying the two painters I hastily leapt astern and turned the pulsating engine around and headed out to the deep. I dropped the anchor, which *this* time had a nice long rope properly attached to an oarlock, and made my first cast towards the shore, where I knew small-mouth and rock bass lurked waiting for their suppers. Gently I reeled my line in, expertly I cast a little to the right of my first spot, I reeled in again, cast in the same spot, reeled, cast and reeled once more. Then, noticing the approaching shoreline, I hauled up the too-light anchor and took a few oar strokes outwards. I started over again.

The sun was setting, the wind getting up and my patience flagging when suddenly I felt a strike. By golly, my line had a beautiful arc! By George, the monster was towing the boat towards the rocks! Well, I played that sucker a good five minutes till he was tired.

Where's the net? Aye, aye, no net! Another five minutes of reeling and releasing foiled my scaly friend and I flipped him into the bow. Meanwhile the lake was getting rougher and the sky darker.

He was a whopper! In his greed, my bass had swallowed the hook, line and sinker and try as I did with bare hands I could not get them out. It leapt helplessly in the bow. To tell the truth, I didn't have rubber gloves, which I find very handy when putting worms on hooks or removing hooks from fish. I had coped without a net, but I didn't have a bonker either.

My flip-flops failed as a substitute for bonking (killing). The bailer, a margarine container, was also too soft. The only hard objects in the boat were the oars! You cannot swing an oar inside a boat on to a flopping fish. Oh, my, that poor, pathetic, flailing fish!

This was not a proud moment.

Not to panic. Quick, start the engine, get my 'trophy' home to a solid piece of wood, or a hammer, by gore, to take him out of his misery. But the engine wouldn't start. It was out of gas.

In amongst the whitecaps I gallantly rowed towards the cottage whilst maintaining vigilance over the frantic fish, for it was flopping furiously. I feared it might actually fly overboard, taking the rod with it. Holy mackerel, it's leaping towards my feet as I row. Heck, I don't like that!

The instinct of self-preservation gave me surprising strength. I thrust my foot out to stop the oncoming enemy, missed it altogether, and succeeded in 'tossing' my flip-flop overboard. Minus a net, I could not catch it before it disappeared.

This is no ordinary flip-flop. I'm sure there isn't another one like it in Canada, except for the one grasped by the toes of my left foot. It comes from the Dominican Republic. In its five-year lifetime it has developed the shape upon its inner sole surface that fits my funny foot, calluses, corns, bunions, and all.

After the fastest row in my long history, I landed, shipped the oars, got out and tied up, did a fifty-yard dash along the dock to a small wood pile, selected a bonker and dashed back to the boat to put him out of his misery (to his and my relief). Then I fetched pliers and gloves and unhooked the big fella, found paper and pencil, traced his outline, cut it out, glued it into the family fish trophy book then, at last, scaled and cleaned him. Phew!

You might be interested in knowing the size and weight of my prize but I didn't actually get these statistics. When I glued the evidence into the trophy book I discovered that he was the smallest small-mouth in the book!

Fishing is not my forte but whenever I do go out in a boat to fish I check that there are on board a net, bonker, gloves, pliers, and gas. After all, you never know when there will be a need to cope with 'a fish out of water'.

Martha

We named her Martha. She's the mother mallard who kept visiting us at 'Shonan' all last summer.

She arrived alone in mid-June, cased the place daily for a couple of weeks, then brought her family, all six of them. We wondered if five of the ducklings were hers and the sixth belonged to someone else. The sixth was the ugly duckling, either ignored or pushed away by the other little ones and their mama. Leaving the laggard behind, they'd take off regularly round five p.m. to visit Whaleback, and then move on to other parts for a bit of exploring. Sometime during the evening, they all returned to Lily Bay to camp under, on or beside our neighbour's dock. That place was popular because it is shallow, usually calm and offers lovely delicacies such as water lilies, arrowheads and other marine plants which shall remain nameless (because I don't know what they're called!).

Every day Martha came to visit us with her family. If our grandchildren were swimming, the ducks swam with them. Certainly neither shy nor frightened, they entertained us and our various visitors constantly.

We have a photo album full of pictures of these beauties with their distinctive blue-purple, white and black-bordered rectangular patch near their tails. This trademark shows up particularly well while the ducks are performing their rigorous primping. There are snaps of Martha alone, on the water, underwater (I know that because I took that photo but it is impossible to decipher; you just have to take my word for it,) and my favourite ones of her bobbing with only the tail in sight – such a funny sight. I once saw a whole shallow bay full of upside-down ducks. In our album there are shots of each of the six offspring, solo and in-group. At least we *think* we have a photo of each one. Who knows?

There are a few extra photos of the ugly duckling for whom we felt special empathy. We tried to figure out how she earned such rotten treatment. Was she from a different tribe, was she a Nosy Parker, did she have halitosis, was she the babbler of the flock, or was she from the other side of the tracks (lake), so to speak?

There is a bothersome problem with Martha's return this year. She has completely forgotten the routine and instead of waiting till 7 or 7:30 a.m. to greet us and tell us to get down here for the ritual skinny dip, she's hailing us and anyone else in the bay who wanted to sleep in, at 5! The first time Earl was really excited, for this was her notifying us that she was back from the long winter sojourn. Immediately Earl wanted to go down to the water and acknowledge her greeting to ensure that she would know how glad we were to have her back safe and sound.

I told him, "No, dear, we have to train her to wait until at least 7. She must learn." Earl happily hopped back into bed for two more hours of sleep. Meanwhile I was in a state of stupor because Martha's nagging had penetrated my dream, making me feel angry at my neighbour for hand-sawing a preposterous pile of pine planks at that ridiculously early hour.

Cleverly, Martha caught on to the routine after a second 5 a.m. one-sided greeting and now she never fails to turn up or let us know she's here at around 7. Sometimes when I go down for my early morning swim Martha has not yet arrived. She is not what you'd call punctual. Nevertheless without fail the moment I open the boathouse door I see her sweet self swimming alongside the shore towards me. Until today I'd had to experience that delightful first morning dip without my cheerful friend. She then hangs around in the sheltered spot beside the boathouse for most of the morning surveying the area, then climbing on to her favourite rock, the same one she used last year, only this time of the year it is just about completely submerged. After grooming she tends to tuck her head under her wing and take a nap.

Martha is a great communicator. When she decides to leave the bay she calls out a couple of "goodbyes" and "see-you-laters" just as she flies by the boathouse and heads west. If she returns during the afternoon she lets out just a few quacks as she passes the boathouse to descend gracefully with a swish into the water.

There have been quite a few times when Martha has brought along a female friend for a good part of the day. Mind you, it's always Martha who gets first dibs on her favourite rock! A couple of times there have been three mallards together, one of whom is easily pushed around – last year's outcast? They never stay more than half a day. Naturally, we wonder what their relationship is to Martha.

A vertical white tail feather makes Martha easy to identify. No amount of grooming flattens this stubborn feather. At the risk of showing my age I must admit that this unique style of hers reminds me of Dennis the Menace's always upwards-thrusting tuft of hair.

Today I'm upset, because my favourite mallard has neither flown into Lily Bay nor swum up from the beach at the bottom of the bay. It is extremely windy and perhaps she simply hasn't the energy to combat the wind and waves. But heck, the thought of spending the remainder of this summer without her friendly flirting and greetings is unbearable.

Have you seen her anywhere? Remember, look for that telltale tall feather.

Better than a croaking frog

There you are, out and about (well not so much out and about as slipping silently) along the surface of a quiet evening's still waters in your stealthy canoe, when you hear a strange sound.

"Wow, what was that!" you're thinking. "I'm sure I just heard distant rumbling. I know it's not thunder, not human either, and not an animal unless perhaps it's a croaking frog, a dying creature, a dog maybe, or a lost bird calling for its mama. Nah, not a bird this; it was very low voiced."

Suddenly I hear an elusive keening cry followed by a couple of sharp yelps.

"Well, maybe it *is* a dog, a sick hound." I even wonder if a mosquito, bent on doing a shallow dive into my ear, is bothering me. They do that, you know, then they feel trapped inside and they squeal and screech.

"No, I must be dreaming." The sound has stopped. Blissful silence. "Besides, it can't possibly be real. I mean, I've never heard anything like this before, and I cannot actually swear that I heard it a minute ago!"

Meanwhile I keep paddling and meditating and guide the canoe towards the shore till I catch a wonderful whiff of lichen as the sun casts its final warm rays on the rocky cliff in front of me. In the peaceful silence I lift my paddle, rest it across the gunwales, and listen briefly to the light splash as drops fall back into the lake off the paddle's blade. Then, silence. Oh, beautiful! That is why I'm here, to listen to the silence.

The mood is disturbed by a groan. This time I realize it is a loon practising a brand new call, one I've never before encountered. I love it. It is long, long, long and low and utterly haunting. "What amazing breath control that bird has," I extol.

Sorry, fella, that's no loon you're listening to as you drift aimlessly in Lake Rosseau's Lily Bay. That's a didgeridoo, one of the oldest wind instruments known to mankind.

If you saw the movie, 'Crocodile Dundee II', you'll have been struck by the didgeridoo's insistent, often sad, mysterious resonance. If you have visited Australia you'll have heard about its use by Aboriginal males and if you attended an educational show by the Aboriginals, you'll have certainly seen and heard it played with reverence and with what seems like an hour-long breath! It is an important part of their culture.

I know that it is for men only and I respect that as much as I can. I did, nevertheless, buy a small didgeridoo to keep as a souvenir. The Aboriginal designs on my didgeridoo are typical of their art, featuring hand-painted colourful lizards, snakes, birds, and a platypus.

No doubt many Muskokans are familiar with the didgeridoo, since many of you have visited Australia. After I came back from Australia with my new didgeridoo I found a great place to display it near my fireplace and left it there. Often I would catch myself admiring it and I sensed that I was secretly longing to play the darn thing. Instead, I would listen to my prize audio cassette called 'Kakadu', composed, arranged and performed by Tony O'Connor. So, one day I picked up the didgeridoo, put it to my mouth, and blew.

Not a sound.

I tried and tried: still not a hint of a sound. I knew it would be hard to play. After many tries, some hyperventilation, a lot of hope and then despair over a period of a few weeks, I put it back in its place to stay. But, you know how it is, my pretty didgeridoo kept beckoning me, and so after about a week more of resistance I tried again, but to no avail.

My didgeridoo is not your typical big, long, heavy hollow eucalyptus 'pipe'. Mine is just 38 inches long and has an inner circumference of 1 inch. It is sometimes called a 'yidaki', the baby member of the didgeridoo family. Playfully, I held the little thing up to my eye as I would a telescope and, well I'll be darned, I didn't see a thing! It was blocked. Blow as I did, I could not clear it. Aha, I fitted the vacuum cleaner tube snugly over the end, and with a simple push of a button the machine inhaled hungrily what must have been several inches of sawdust and perhaps a termite or two. I could hear the stuff getting sucked in – quite a rewarding noise. At my next peek I saw daylight without dust. I blew again and nearly passed out for my breath escaped rapidly and silently straight through the instrument.

Little by little, with variations of breath pressure and different tongue movements, I got sounds resembling the kind of music I was longing for. My lungs expanded considerably, for I could only achieve success by using extremely long exhalations.

Poor, long-suffering Earl has had to listen to my amateurish blows, gasps and wails for months. Guests have politely listened. Sarah's dog howls in response, and my son's dog is terrified and tries to attack my didgeridoo, much as she attacks the hose when it is spraying.

Then, home came our daughter Jessie from a year-long tour of Australia and New Zealand armed with *her* spanking new, enormous didgeridoo. She also brought a cassette of didgeridoo music and booklet of instructions. How puzzled our Pierrefonds neighbours must have been by the weird sounds emitting from our back yard as she and I played our precious instruments on the heady evening of her return. Hers had a deeper tone than mine, quite lovely (we thought).

In Muskoka, Jessie and I would sit on deck chairs on the dock and practise. We'd try saying the alphabet through it. We'd try animal sounds. Sometimes my husband would put down his book, pick up his fishing rod and disappear out of earshot in *Peewee*. After a half-hour of fishing, he'd return to two exhausted family members with very sore mouths and funny lines above and to the sides of their lips. Jessie ended up with a bruised chin and a sore foot from supporting the heavy instrument in between her big toe and the next toe, as she sat with her legs stretched out and propped on a stool. My little 'yidaki' didn't reach my feet but it did rest in my hands and sometimes I caught myself actually raising a finger now and then as though I were playing the recorder. There are no holes along the didgeridoo other than the openings at the mouth and the bottom end.

Our daily didgeridoo sessions by the shore of Lake Rosseau were great fun (for us), and Earl got a real kick out of our facial expressions and weird wails. There was certainly more laughter than music. That was then; this is now. A winter has passed and I have learned how to do the circular or 'round' breathing; that is, making a continuous sound while breathing both in and out. I can play my didgeridoo!

My thanks go to my younger son's friend who came to my house to show me how to get started. He had me filling my cheeks with so much air they ached for days – I truly had stiff cheeks. He told me to blow through my didgeridoo into a bucket of water so that I could watch the bubbles and see if they became constant. It took a long time to achieve the constancy whereby bubbles, smaller ones admittedly, appeared even while I was inhaling. I also tried it with a straw in a glass of water.

Then Matt's friend invited me to attend a didgeridoo workshop, promising me that in addition to five eager male students he had found a couple of girls who also wanted lessons. Such was my ambition that I drove to his mother's house in our worst snowstorm of the winter. Upon arrival I learned that I was the only female, as well as the only person not in his/her thirties (and far from it!).

I had a blast. They were real gentlemen, and it was delightful sharing our spiritual awe of the instrument and its history. With the instructor's guidance and with other eager participants huffing and puffing nearby, you cannot help but get the round breathing after two steady hours of practising. Interspersed, of course, with laughter and some raspberry-like sounds, funny bubble noises, plus a few splashes.

This summer my neighbours in Lily Bay will have to put up with much didgeridooing, but with less shrieky mistakes. Maybe they will learn to enjoy the magic of the didgeridoo when they hear a variety of amazing calls and feel hints of rhythm exiting from my hollow Australian Aboriginal 'yidaki'.

Maybe, it will sound better than a croaking frog.

A backwards boater

Being neither a water nymph nor a parallel parker on land, I cannot fathom the logic of turning the boat's steering wheel towards the dock while shooting backwards. In fact, the last time I tried to dock at Wallace Marine my brain balked entirely at transmitting this message to my hands. Instead, it bypassed them and told the boat to stall. Thus, as easily as eating blueberry pie, I paddled her to the gas dock, threw a painter to the worried 'gas boy' (our daughter's summer job one year,) hopped (well, uh, clambered) on to terra firma, requested a fill-up of both of the red plastic gas tanks taking up too much room in the little boat, and then strode nonchalantly to the little shop at the other end of the dock.

The Mercury outboard is easily recognized by its sort of shuddering sound, especially my very old, temperamental one. Always moments before my faded 14-foot Peterborough, the venerable *Blue Champagne*, speeds into view of Wallace Marine, heads would automatically turn. I could feel the tension all the way out as I got opposite Clevelands. The mechanic would hastily put down his tools and the gas boy would shade his eyes while following my erratic approach. Usually Irv, sometimes Richard (Wallace), would reconnoitre the situation on the docks trying to guess which spot I'd pick this time and prepare to make a dash to 'help me dock'. That's the polite way of saying 'prevent a crash, damaged boats and docks, maybe lawsuits, and a squashed hand or two.'

The trouble is that there was not one dock long enough to permit my making a nice neat landing and often there would be a boat tied up at each and every mooring ring but one, leaving what seemed a tiny spot between an antique mahogany monster and a spanking new Oliver. They teased me relentlessly at Wallace's but I knew they enjoyed being valiant. You can't beat the dry, good humour of the Muskokan.

A greater challenge for the novice boater is docking at the Port Carling docks on the Lake Rosseau side. Just try to squeeze your boat into a slip built for two with waves rocking your boat, the other boat already in the slip and the floating dock you're trying to reach. Shiver my timbers, how do people manage that with big boats?

Port Carling is a lovely place but there are so many people, dogs and boats coming and going at dockside that you can't expect someone to notice your difficulties and lend you a helping hand – especially if he values his hand! To add insult to injury, you invariably stumble the moment you start walking on the big wharf, even nimble teenagers do, for the old boards are thinner than the new boards they've used to replace the rotting ones.

At least it's a whole lot easier to get your gas at MacLennan's in Port Carling than at Windermere. No way would I approach the short pier there under power!

I prefer to pole myself in, like a gondolier.

What the Wallaces must have wondered that time when my boat paid them a little visit, having crossed the lake from Tobin's Island, skirted the rocks with the flashing light, kept within the two buoys in the area opposite Paignton House, passed the water-ski jump at Clevelands, and hence arrived safe and sound – all the while proceeding (or should I say receding?) *backwards*! I just knew that Irv was going to make a remark, yet again, about my driving when my son yelled to him from the stern, "How d'you get this thing into forward?"

Of course, it was just another case of ordering a small part. "Come back tomorrow," Irv said, his face taut as he tried to choke back the snorts and hoots that followed when I was mostly out of earshot.

"Backwards . . . again?"

Now I've graduated from the little boat to the big one, a 20-foot Crestliner with I/O engine – or from the ridiculous to the sublime. It was hard enough to remember in *Blue Champagne* to: 1) squeeze the bump on the gas hose twice lightly; 2) move the small black lever (the throttle?) all the way forward; 3) press the small, black button (the choke?); 4) at the same time turn the key, and hold my breath.

Now I have to remember to: 1) turn on the blower; 2) wait; 3) pull out the lever and pump it forward and downward twice; 4) turn the key; 5) then, when I think the engine is warmed up, put the lever in the perpendicular position to let it engage; 6) press the little red tilt button on the lever's handle; 7) squeeze the orange switch under the same dang lever's handle in order to get into reverse or forward; 8) and when moving the big lever, do it gently; 9) turn off the blower.

I prefer to row; yes, facing *backwards* . . . again!

A night at the theatre

We were ready. We'd been cottage owners for five years and owners of a decent boat for one, and we'd practised the run in daylight a million times. Boating to Port Carling had become routine, since we went there for booze, groceries and doctor's appointments on a regular basis anyway.

What gave us the final push to attempt the trip to Port Carling at night was Araby Lockhart, bless her heart! She, whom I'd known in my youth, had the lead in the current play, thus prompting my nostalgic desire to meet her again.

Besides, it was time!

In the morning Earl and I took our normal route via Cayley's Cut to town. During the return voyage, going exactly the same route, we charted our course. With pen in hand I wrote down every change of direction as it showed on the compass, and how long we stayed in that direction and at what r.p.m. we were cruising. Because I have never achieved competence in driving the big boat, I 'won' the job as navigator. It became a heavy responsibility for me to tell my husband where to go!

At times I have received words of praise for my instinctive knowledge of north, south, east and west. This skill I actually acquired from growing up in Toronto, where the lake was always to the south. As a genuine water baby I could always sense the lake's location. When I was a teenager my solace had been my Sunday bike ride from the top of the Avenue Road hill down to the waterfront to watch the water. There I dreamed of such achievements as passing grade eleven, going to Muskoka in the summer, becoming the mascot of the Toronto Maple Leafs, and owning a sailboat.

We did another dry run at noon, during which my husband tried not to watch where he was going by keeping his eyes on the compass and r.p.m. gauge, while obeying my instructions only. We did it once more in the afternoon, going off course only to gas up at Wallace's.

Evening fell and with it a few drops of rain. The trip to Port Carling was undertaken in daylight, as we were invited to dinner at Edenvale Inn by my cousin. At this dinner, which we ate under an umbrella while gentle rain splashed around us, both my cousin and I disgraced ourselves by squeezing our slippery barbecued ribs so hard they squirted out of our fingers and landed, plop, in the middle of our white blouses. Our trip to the washroom and complete removal of our blouses to hold the red spots under running water produced no improvement. In fact, it added a grey, wet stain to the picture plus a tendency to make our blouses stick to the skin in obvious places.

Sitting in the dark at the theatre I was truly inspired by the play and Araby's stellar performance. Unfortunately, since neither Earl nor I had a jacket or sweatshirt with us I decided not to visit Araby backstage after all.

My cousin, at least, was able to cover up her disgrace with a light, summer jacket. What that meant was that we left the theatre immediately after the play, leaving my cousins behind to mingle with the crowd and meet Araby, the lucky dogs.

It was a black night.

Rain, rain, rain! I had to read my instructions by putting my head outside and holding them close to the light. We didn't have a flashlight, just a floodlight.

It was the most hair-raising boat trip I've ever undertaken. Islands kept popping up everywhere, islands I swear I'd never seen in daylight. The shoreline, when we caught it with the floodlight, was completely askew, and the faint landmark lights were all in the wrong places. In my first attempt to use my detailed instructions the rain caused the ink to run, and turned the piece of paper into a soggy, shredded mess.

We were travelling blind! Brave Earl drove very slowly, until we finally sighted Woodmere's flag and boathouse light. What a relief! Then in no time we picked up the reliable lights in the Cut. From then on it was smooth sailing, since once past a very familiar buoy it was an absolute straight course to our cottage. How grateful we were to those cottagers who turned on their boathouse and dock lights that night to keep us safe!

That night at the theatre taught us some valuable lessons: to carry a flashlight, jacket and pencil in the boat at all times, and to avoid barbecued ribs on theatre outings.

I hope Araby comes back another year in another play!

Knitting novices in Muskoka

If my brother and his male cousin were able to learn to knit earmuffs, of all things, at the tender age of eight, then you'd think an adult female would be able to pick it up effortlessly. Right? In my brother's case, he *had* to knit. What else was he going to do, stuck as he was at Juddhaven, admonished to behave, be quiet and be still while his parents and aunt and uncle had their regular afternoon snoozes?

Fortunately, that experience hasn't turned my brother off Muskoka. The enforced knitting was a kind of trade-off. In return for their being able to prove to the grown-ups that indeed they had stayed on that veranda and knitted their earmuffs, they got to sail, fish and swim the rest of the time.

The two cousins have not knitted a single sock, scarf or sweater since. The adult female in question (my daughter, Sarah) has more or less mastered the craft, but in the process she suffered from calluses on her fingers and shortage of breath. Watching her I noticed she tried to hold her breath for a complete row. No wonder she was exhausted! Furthermore, her crackling wrist joints made more noise than her clicking needles did. Adding insult to injury, Sarah informed me the morning after her first full evening of knitting solo that she even had a sore heel. Come on now, Sarah! Actually, I had noticed that while holding her breath and clenching her teeth, she had kept her legs crossed with one foot planted extra firmly on the floor. It's a wonder it didn't go right through!

In order for her to learn how to knit, we had each bought wool and the same pattern book so that if there were problems we could confer on the phone. Mind you, I had to pay frequent visits to her house when something went drastically wrong.

You have to understand that starting out with ribbing, one plain, one pearl, while using multi-coloured wool is already a challenge. Sarah truly could not see the difference between the two stitches. If she put her knitting down, even just to plug in the kettle, she would return to it and be unable to determine what her last stitch was. It does get easier to recognize after you've knitted a couple of inches, but it certainly is discouraging until you get there.

Perhaps it would have been wiser to start my nearly-novice knitter off with something simple, like a hot water bottle cover – boring! Back in January, when the air temperature kept hovering around minus 15 degrees, Sarah's two schnauzers pretty well begged her to make them each a sweater, or else! If ever there was pressure for her to learn, that was it.

Well, I finished my sweater, but Kaylie refused wear it, *period!* Sure, she slept on it happily enough, but she refused to budge whenever Sarah put it on her. This didn't come as a complete surprise because not once had she agreed to wear a store-bought one. They either didn't fit or were too stiff or 'scratchy'.

But my sweater was perfect. Couldn't Kaylie see that?

Maggie, who doesn't have a problem wearing sweaters, is still waiting for her hand-knitted one. When Sarah comes to Muskoka this summer for her vacation she's going to have to sit on the deck every afternoon while I have my nap and knit, knit and knit just like my brother did, until she finishes Maggie's sweater.

My poor daughter, the first time I set out to teach her to knit we had (or, rather, I had) decided on making lopi sweaters, since everybody told me that because of the heavy, thick wool and fat knitting needles, "they knit up fast". Hogwash! Good knitters made it sound as though the sweaters actually knit themselves.

I must admit that the special waterproof (sort of) Icelandic wool is amazing. There we were, the two of us sitting on the dock enjoying the sun, large needles clacking, sometimes swatting mosquitoes or pesky no-see-em's, deep into a discussion about the dinner menu, while Sarah kept interrupting with violent sneezes. Supposedly, the hay fever season was finished and until we'd taken up our knitting she had not displayed the slightest sign of coming down with a cold. As we both continued to knit, she continued to sneeze, then cough, and then she wheezed. She was having an asthma attack. When I took my eyes off my knitting, I noticed that she was sitting in a shaft of sunlight, the kind that captures every speck of dust in its magnetic force. What did I see? Oh, dear, millions and millions of short, stiff hairs in magic colours flitting about all around her. Observing her in the extraordinary light I wondered how she could even see, let alone breathe.

Needless to say, that was the end of Sarah's first attempt at knitting. Guess who got to finish her lopi sweater? Indeed, I have three wonderful daughters and I ended up finishing four lopi sweaters before knitting one for my brother – the one of earmuffs fame.

For me, the beauty of knitting lopi sweaters is that they make the seven hour drive from Pierrefonds to Muskoka seem like only couple of hours. Furthermore, the most tedious part of knitting any sweater is the sleeves, and I can do a whole one in that trip. Because the wool is so hot, hairy and heavy, I learned not to knit in the sun in the summer and to confine myself to doing it only in the air-conditioned car. Quite a few trips to Toronto and I had the back done – great!

Who am I to try to teach someone else how to knit? Having finished my first lopi sweater on my fortieth birthday in July, my deadline date, I was very proud of myself. It was too hot to wear it in the summer, of course, but it would be perfect for the fall. Meanwhile I'd brought up Sarah's unfinished lopi and was looking forward to doing its second sleeve on the trip back to Pierrefonds. When I presented it to her, she thanked me, said it was beautiful – it *was*! Earl took a photo of the two of us in our hand-knitted lopis, and that was that.

Well, um, my friend who is an expert knitter and my original teacher, praised me vociferously when gazing at Sarah and me

113

standing side by side in our precious lopis. Suddenly she burst out laughing and pointed her waving finger at the sleeves of Sarah's 'masterpiece'.

Jumping jellyfish, each sleeve had a different design! I had simply used my own pattern on the trip home instead of hers. You see, there is a great variety of designs among lopi sweaters. They're all Fair Isles, yes, but not identical. They strongly resemble each other but are actually different if you take a close look. That is, ahem, if you are an expert.

Sarah, good sport that she is, would not allow me to rip it out because, as she put it, her sweater is unique; it's got that personal touch. No doubt she feared that I'd never finish another doggone sleeve, anyway.

She could have been right.

There've been other knitting fiascos in my career in crafts. The first socks I ever knitted on four needles, a huge challenge, were so big that they became bed-socks. My grandchildren have all benefited (?) from receiving adorable newborn outfits and later on, vests. The vests were easy and quick, definitely the ideal choice for, of course, they have *no sleeves*. There have been, perhaps, a few too many scarves and mittens and too few sweaters. Now all the leftover balls of wool are taking shape and looking extremely colourful. Some poor soul in my family will be glad I didn't throw those scattered skeins away, for the new patchwork blanket I'm knitting will surely save someone from suffering from hypothermia some day.

I have to finish it first. All it will take is a fine summer in Muskoka. And some spare time.

Getting a kick out of kayaking

Shush, nobody knows this, but the Backward Boater is letting you in on a big secret, one that can revamp your life and your figure, too, even if you are past muddle (no, not a spelling error) age. Now her 'abs' are strong, her biceps bulging and her front female feature (never a threat to Marilyn Munro) starting to sag somewhat less, sort of.

Stop it right there. Your "ahems" and hoots are interrupting the thought process needed to continue writing this analysis of rejuvenation. Surely you've heard of poetic licence and you know that a hint of exaggeration is good for the health.

Oh ye boat-lovers, there is revolutionary news for you. Those adorable, colourful kayaks, some with the brand name

'Cricket', that have started dotting the Muskoka Lakes, are here to stay. They don't pollute, don't produce wake that destroys the shoreline and disturbs nesting loons and they don't create sound – unless you count shrieks of joy as noise pollution. Furthermore, the new affordable kayaks are so light that they are easy to lift and launch solo, even for seniors.

Though the new-style kayaks come in many colours, shapes and sizes and with a variety of names, they all share the asset of being veritable floating exercise machines that are fabulous for the upper body muscles, including the ones you use for smiling.

Please understand that they do not replace the canoe in my heart, yet both are equally special watercraft which allow us to sit at water level – heavenly! In addition, both are silent, odour free, nature-friendly, and good-looking to boot. Granted, they differ in that the modern kayak cannot be described as having a classic look. The Lordly canoe and the Princely, plastic kayak share another feature, however, as both require some skill and balance to get in and out of. As for safety, the kayak, unlike the canoe, cannot tip over in the water even with someone aboard. It won't sink either.

Even a child can quickly master the technique for stroking with the unique double sided paddle. Once one has established a paddling rhythm using a comfortable grip, water stops dribbling half way down the shaft and landing on one's lap. Strength is not a major requirement; style helps. You can use kayaks in rough water – just ask my grandson, eleven-year-old Cole, who braved the cold wind and rain last Thanksgiving weekend, and landed only to change into dry clothing and go right back out over and over again.

If you are going with the wind you can stop stroking altogether and float peacefully along. What a way and place to relax!

As balance is involved you need to use a special knack to step on to or off the kayak, unless you are in very shallow water. While the kayak won't tip over, *you* might! Part of the problem is that there are no handles, thwarts, or edges to grasp. However, Earl and I discovered that a dock ladder is just the thing. By going down a few rungs and holding on to the ladder, you can then lower yourself into the kayak's carved out seat section, which is concave and comfy rather than high and scary. People with balance problems can easily get aboard and off this way. Once seated you feel as though you are actually sitting down in the water instead of on top of it. It's awesome, and the backrest is sloped so that you feel like taking a nap instead of a paddle. It *has* to be good for sore backs! Your feet even rest in appropriately designed indentations.

Okay, okay, the smidgen of a confession is due. After your first few outings you might feel stiffness in those muscles that haven't had a workout in (could it be?) months. Also, be aware that a novice might grip the lengthy paddle too hard at first, causing the fingers to complain later on. Relax. The aches do dissipate and won't return if you keep kayaking.

How did our love affair with the Crickets begin? One afternoon in September while I was swimming in Lily Bay and Earl was watching loons from the deck of the boathouse, two kayaks, one brilliant red and the other sunflower yellow, came by going at a nifty clip. You can easily make them go very fast if you want. Breathtaking!

Our neighbours from down the shore south of Laura Point were out for a stroll, so to speak, for that's how it feels when you slow down. They chatted with me as I bobbed in the water beside them. As they sat so low in the water our heads were almost at the same level. Conversing was easy. Earl beckoned them to come closer so that he could have a chat and look as well.

And, well, one thing led to another and we accepted their kind invitation to help ourselves any time to try them out. 'Any time' became the next day. Earl's kayak, very easy to spot on the lake, just had to be called *Flame*. Mine is a psychedelic mix of greens and purples, fondly nicknamed *Jiminy*.

My New Year's resolution might come back to haunt me, but I bet I'll be really fit and slim by midsummer next year. Who knows, after weeks of practice and conditioning, one fine day Earl and I just might paddle all the way around Tobin Island in our colourful Crickets.

Maybe we'd better re-activate our cellular phone!

What rocks these?

Have you noticed the lovely, man-made rock formations that have been popping up mysteriously in Muskoka? Is this a recent phenomenon peculiar to Muskoka, or have they been appearing elsewhere, say, on Lake of Bays, Lake Vernon or in Algonquin Park? And why now?

There were two last year on Tobin Island's Laura Point. I used to paddle by and admire them. To tell the truth, I was a tiny bit scared of them, for I didn't know what they were for and by whom they were built.

With difficulty I would manage to get the canoe and myself into just the right position to photograph them, with the sun behind me and the water nice and calm. I succeeded in snapping a few shots, taken from various angles so that the structures showed up clearly displaying their grace and interesting human-form silhouettes. Out of curiosity I checked the number of stones used in each and learned that there was not a definite formula. I've seen a couple of headless ones, and still found them beautiful, too.

It was unfortunate that I had finished my film before I had a chance to scoot across the lake and find some more to capture on film. Actually, I considered myself lucky to have been able to take any pictures of these stone sculptures at all, since sunny moments last summer were rare. I knew that without the sun I couldn't do them justice, made as they were of the typical Muskoka grey-pink stone, perched alone on exposed flat grey-pink rock and usually without a dark background to serve as contrast.

Since I'm not remotely handy, I chose to wait till my return to Montreal to have Earl remove the film from the camera. Imagine my suspense waiting to see and show the artistic photos!

Although I was told otherwise, my camera is not completely idiot-proof. With this camera you *can* safely take 36 shots, jerking the lever after each one, without taking a picture on top of another at least! Each time, the tiny number at the side moves a number higher. At '36' the lever sticks. That's when I need my husband – for rewinding, clicking and removing.

Need I say more? There was no film in the camera! To make matters worse, the Laura Point formations were gone when I returned this spring.

What would you figure these figures signify? Would you be superstitious about approaching one, touching one, or taking its picture? Last summer I badly wanted to build my own in my bay, but I wondered if they were used by the Inuit or our Native People to mark an area for a land claim, or attack, or civil disobedience. These worries probably stemmed from my living not too far from Oka, Quebec.

I feel the utmost respect for these marvels and their creators.

Because I had noticed new ones showing up in different locations for the last two springs, I decided that they were built during the winter. But how could that be? Wouldn't the rocks be buried under snow? Maybe they were used, I thought, in order to mark the location of an angler's personal ice-fishing hole. Then I ran out of ideas altogether.

Now I know that they are called *inukshuk*, an Inuit word meaning 'something acting in the capacity of a man'. The Inuit use them primarily to aid in hunting, by placing them strategically to scare caribou herds into narrow valleys where the hunters await them. Many of today's hunters use *inukshuks* that were built by their ancestors. The same applies to *inukshuks* that serve as landmarks for sled and boat navigation in the Arctic.

If you're cruising around Lake Rosseau the end of this summer and turn into Lily Bay of Tobin's Island, you'll discover a brand new *inukshuk*. It will be standing on our own Gibraltar, a stone's throw from 'Shonan'.

Watching wildlife at the cottage

Martha is back, plus a host of other interesting visitors.

True to her form of the last three years, Martha, our favourite mallard, enthusiastically greets us whenever she flies past the boathouse, arriving for a chat and pieces of stale bread. As her penetrating persistent quacks are hard to ignore, Earl and I obediently get up from chairs or the bed to rush down to her chosen corner of Lily Bay, right beside the boathouse.

Let's go back a bit. This is her territory, no doubt about it, but when she had failed to make her appearance by mid-June, we befriended Maurice. Then he started bringing along a couple of his pals on a steady basis. Eventually he and another drake took to hanging out in Lily Bay, and Earl and I began to fret:

"What if Martha doesn't come? What if the bossy drakes keep her away?"

Hurrah! Martha quacked her way back into our lives and has started keeping regular company with the handsome Maurice. Figuring he owned both us and the protected spot on the east side of our boathouse, Maurice was reluctant to let Martha get close. Well, c'mon, Martha is now and always will be our number-one wild duck and it didn't take Earl long to straighten this out with Maurice. With scary looks and noises and a waving paddle in his hand, he managed to teach the fellow some manner, specifically, to wait for his turn.

After Martha has finished filling herself with our treats – I wonder if she fully appreciates the fact that the bread is baked in our own bread oven – she climbs up on to the rock nearby to sunbathe and survey the entire bay. She's looking for loons, of course, so she can warn the other ducks. Without apparent vocal communication, we see the frightened drakes also clamber out of the water to safety the moment a loon ventures into the bay.

Looking like a covey of lawyers and judges in court with their chief witness, Martha, they assess the situation. For their beautiful bright orange legs and feet, they have to be admired as well as for the gasoline-green 'wigs' displayed on their heads and sparkling as they make movements in the sunlight. As for Martha, she may never be as colourful as her male counterparts but she has a way of nonchalantly showing off her delicate femininity with her long, graceful, slender neck that is quite a contrast to the thicker male necks.

The great blue heron has done a few Marcel Marceau skits on rocks and docks in Lily Bay, but he has completely ignored his friend of other years, the *inukshuk*. During the last three years he has paid at least a couple of visits to the rock sentinel standing at attention on top of Lily Bay's Gibraltar. Oh, well, he'll probably come back.

At dusk an owl flew towards us as we stood on our boathouse deck, then flapped his big wings to carry him up and over the roof. It was easy, even in the half-light, to identify him because of his squat body and the way his wings fluttered like sheets of newspaper in the wind. Thrilling! We'd heard owls calling many times but never seen them in flight.

A merganser swam by with two babies in her wake. That was a tiny family compared with what we usually see – a bit disappointing.

One time, Earl called me to the deck rail to identify an object coming towards us in the water. When it got close we saw its colour, brown, its solid, chunky body and had a good view of its head above the water. It really could have been mistaken for a dog except for its ears being well rounded. Once we learned that muskrats eat fish, we knew that the swimming animal was the same fellow who had taken up residence in our boathouse previously, leaving much evidence. He'd better not like tiny tykes' toes!

The same must be said of the eighteen-inch diameter turtle we've seen in the water below our lower deck and resting on a large flat rock near the water's edge. Obviously not enjoying being stared at by our guests, he slid back into safer territory, the lake. That same day my husband, a great tease, called to me as I was swimming to the ladder to get out. "Don't come this way! Go away!" Of course I didn't take him seriously at first, but did I turn away fast when I saw the object he was pointing at a foot to my right, the head and scrawny neck of 'the snapper'. One more critter to worry about when our grandchildren come here for vacation!

Our son Matt, a herpetologist, has tried to reassure us that turtles may, just may, snap at us if feeling threatened while they're on land but not if they are in their own safe territory, the water. Hope he's right!

Spring peepers serenaded us in June but now they've gone. How wonderful it would be to hear frogs croaking in our bay. Now the only place I hear that sound is in Baron's gift shop in Port Carling when I walk past the fake ones.

Loons continue to call, thank goodness, especially in the evening. Crows caw and something stutters in the woods sometimes. Would it be a quail, or perhaps a partridge, or a pheasant?

The best has been saved for the last. When my cousin Jenny from Norway Point was having dinner with us last week, she looked across the bay from the boathouse and joyfully cried, "There are two deer on Laura Point." What a wonderful sight! The pair of small does, no longer white spotted but still young and very thin, stepped sure-footed on the mostly rocky surface about thirty feet above the shoreline. Stopping to pluck a bit of vegetation now and then, they whisked their tails jerkily, but kept them pointing up the rest of the time looking altogether confident. Certainly they were not aware of our presence on the opposite shore.

I said, "I hope they go down to the lake for a drink. I have never seen them drink in my life." Earl and Jenny hadn't either and, lo and behold, didn't those two sandy coloured does go down to the lake, one behind the other. The first placed her hooves in the water and gently bent down to drink. Slowly she moved in deeper followed by her companion, who was also thirsty. We were enthralled.

As if seeing them drink weren't enough, the two little deer proceeded to entertain us further, the one in front always being in control. She lifted her head, looked around, tested the water's depth and continued straight ahead, cooling herself off in the deeper water. The other watched as the leader had a long swim, swimming towards our shore but turning around, perhaps to encourage her friend. Now she also ventured forward into deep water and swam out towards her playmate. About twenty feet from shore they met and appeared to frolic together going back and forward towards and away from one another.

What a vision we enjoyed, two graceful heads in the water with their distinctive ears pointing at forty-five degree angles. After enjoying a ten-minute swim they returned to shore and climbed effortlessly back on the long rock, shook themselves, then continued on through the trees and out of sight around the tip of the point. Unforgettable!

Nevertheless let's hope our photos captured the magic.

Earl's passion

If you had grown up in Africa surrounded by exotic, tropical plants you would understand my husband's reaction when he rediscovered the Passion Flower nearly fifty years after leaving his home. There they were, hundreds of bright, three-dimensional, multi-coloured flowers covering the fences alongside the streets leading to our rented studio apartment in Port Grimaud in the south of France.

What a beautiful flower, with its contrasting purple, white, deep blue, yellow and burnt orange parts!

The photos do not lie. Its tiny, tawny, tenacious tendrils dangle everywhere, looking like little girls' ringlets. They coil around each other, around the basket's edges, around the hanging hook and sometimes I swear they are grasping my baby finger as I examine them.

After returning to Canada, Earl described his discovery to our family. To tell the truth, his excitement was contagious, although I did have to admire his photos of these beauties every single time he showed them off to anyone who would look or listen.

Somebody *had* listened. Our daughter Jessie gave him a Passion Flower plant for Father's Day. Life has not been the same since. This husband of mine, never remotely interested in our garden in Pierrefonds nor in cutting and fertilizing the grass, weeding or mulching, now visits his precious plant every morning even before his first cup of coffee. Every day. What's he doing? He's counting new flowers or searching for new buds, watering it, pruning it, feeding it, gazing at it. For all I know, he may even be talking to it!

Hanging over the laundry tub in our basement for easy draining in front of a sunny window and under a grow light, the Passion Flower plant has wintered successfully in Pierrefonds twice already. When we go away during the 'off' season, does Earl worry about frozen pipes or break-ins? No, he worries about his plant. Fortunately, our wonderful neighbours go down to our basement daily to take care of it during our absences.

The hardest part about Earl's big vine, for that is what it is even though it lives in a hanging basket, is transporting it to and from Muskoka, for it takes up a lot of room. Still, if he takes his Passion Flower up to Muskoka every year I get to take up my planter boxes full of rosemary, thyme, basil, parsley, and dill.

That's a fair trade-off, don't you think?

Up here at the cottage his two Passion Flowers – Jessie gave him another one this year – get moved in and out of the sun, and in and out of the wind, as they hang over the upper deck of our boathouse. They do keep Earl hopping. Oddly, the vine Jessie gave him this year has yet to bloom. Heck, it once sprouted one bud and that has disappeared. Well, after perusing some information he found on the Internet, Earl learned that some Passion Flowers take six years to flower.

Can we wait that long? Let's face it, in some ways it's riskier than buying green bananas.

Late last fall, Jessie warned me that a package from California addressed to her father would be arriving in Pierrefonds before Christmas. I was instructed to keep it hidden until Christmas day then hand it over to him. I received these instructions while carefully reading a recipe for Pecan Lace cookies and beating eggs at the same time.

Well ah, um, I hate to admit this, but it behooves me to confess that one of my many shortcomings is memory lapse. You think you know the rest, but you don't. Okay, I did forget all about Jessie's warning when a certain small package arrived at our door in Pierrefonds via courier with no description of contents, no revealing return address and feeling light and definitely dangerous.

This occurred during the anthrax scare.

Gingerly, I pressed the package. It rustled, it felt distinctly weird – exactly like anthrax, I swear. I didn't even want to bring it into the house. I called the police, who weren't that interested to begin with. I next mentioned the fact that our MNA, for my husband has always campaigned loyally and actively for him, wouldn't be pleased with the police's lack of concern. I threatened to inform our favourite radio station, *CJAD* and *The Gazette*.

A tall, slightly perplexed police officer finally turned up at my door without so much as one blare of his sirens. Heck! After donning rubber gloves, he fingered the mysterious packet, smelled it and jiggled it while I stepped well back hoisting my sweater up over my mouth and nose and placing my glasses over my eyes. Next, he placed it on our dining room table. *What was he thinking?* We'd never be able to eat off that table again. Then he reluctantly put it in a bag and prepared to leave with it. I had to beg him to let us know what was inside the brown paper wrapping.

Later we learned through our own perseverance (and a bit more name-dropping), that they had destroyed the parcel unopened. What a let-down!

My let-down after phoning Jessie in St. Catharines to tell her about our adventure, was far worse. I still feel deep regret and shame. Jessie had ordered through the Internet a package of seeds for several varieties of the Passion Flower complete with growing instructions to be sent to her dad for Christmas.

What has the Passion Flower got to do with Muskoka? You may well ask. Well, you too can experience the joy of nurturing a Passion Flower plant that, if you're lucky, will give you new blooms nearly every day, as others close up within a day or two. The different varieties have fabulous colours and charming names, such as the 'Constance Elliot'. If the nurseries up here don't have any perhaps you can persuade one to obtain them.

Wolf howl in Algonquin Park

There've been other big events in my life besides getting married and having five babies awesome enough to make me recognize that mine has not been an ordinary life. But I cannot stop yet. I've never seen a whale.

Skiing down Engleberg (in Switzerland) on a sunny December day was exciting enough, but what put that day into my top ten category was the typical sound of a Swiss cowbell's tinkling. I looked way down and saw a small herd being led back to its barn, for lunch maybe or milking. In the crisp mountain air that was music to match a loon call in Muskoka.

Snorkelling off the Great Barrier Reef is another once-in-a-lifetime experience. I saw, swam with and almost touched a cornucopia of saltwater fish of dazzling colours and shapes. Those shower curtains and posters you've seen do not lie!

Last summer's main event took place one night in August in Algonquin Park. It should be easy to guess what I'm talking about but you wouldn't dream that the most extraordinary feature of my 'wolf howl' was the silence.

Picture this: you're in a 25 kilometre-long convoy of 670 vehicles following each other on a winding, narrow Highway 60 through wilderness country in the dead of night being waved on here and there by a warden bearing a torch. There are no fender benders, no jumping jacks jockeying for a more advanced position in the slow moving line – even despite the request at the earlier talk at the Algonquin Park outdoor theatre that we drive almost bumper to bumper. The excitement amongst the passengers of all the cars, trucks and vans is nearly at fever pitch, and yet you're either silent or merely whispering. The drive took about half an hour, and during that time all regular traffic was being held at both ends of the park to allow all the 670 vehicles to reach their positions.

At the outdoor theatre after the informative and interesting slide show on wolves, Dan Strickland had admonished us to be absolutely quiet once parked, not to shuffle our feet on the loose gravel as we descend from our vehicles, to close our doors silently without even a click, and to avoid the disturbance of children's cries and dog's barks by shutting them inside our cars with windows closed (only a tiny opening allowed for air). Knowing how noisy a zipper sounds in the still of the night at campsites, we even zipped or unzipped our jackets while still inside the car.

All this stealth increased our sense of adventure.

Waiting outside in the chilly air along with about 2664 other people I felt humbled by the majesty of the silence shared. Suddenly my daughter Liv poked me and, *wow*, I heard them – way, way off in the distance. Maybe what I heard the first time was a warden calling the wolves, you can't tell the difference, but when I heard more howls and yelps from both adults and pups, I knew I was listening to the real thing. This was well worth the hours spent between leaving our cottage on Lake Rosseau at 5 p.m. and assembling with nature lovers like ourselves to enjoy one of nature's wonders, wolves howling in the night. The calls lasted no more than a couple of minutes; obviously, you had to be listening hard at precisely the right moment.

In all, during a stretch of one and a half hours, we listened to three series of wolf calls. Twice in between, the wardens at each end of the Park allowed traffic to drive through. As cars drove past us I wondered if they knew what was going on and how much they appreciated having to wait to be allowed to proceed with their journeys. Some of those waiting at the East gate might have been lucky enough to hear the wolves, too. They had to be astounded, at least, by the silence of 2664 people!

An added bonus was the display of Aurora Borealis. By the time we returned to Lake Rosseau at 3:30 a.m. the Northern Lights were spectacular, celebrating an unforgettable night of silent camaraderie, wolf howls and a light show.

Seagulls' supper

What was my number one priority at the cottage for the new millenium: read *War and Peace*, swim 100 strokes every day, learn to swim the butterfly, get up and stay up on my windsurfer, meditate, build a new dock, a raft, or a canoe, or (heaven forbid!) write the Great Canadian Novel?

Believe it or not, that last suggestion was my number two priority and number one was to welcome Martha back again this summer. Until she finally arrived I was constantly on the lookout for her and her mate and babies, but not for the 29 other mallards she brought along with her to Lily Bay a few times last summer! Sure, I wanted the blue heron to come back for a chat with my *inukshuk*, and I'd have adored a visit from a merganser family, and of course I wanted my family, grandchildren, cousins, and friends to come. That goes without saying.

Still, welcoming Martha was top of the list.

There I'd be at the end of June sitting on the dock looking and listening for her, especially for that swish sound she makes as she glides on top of the water, like a water skier tipping up his skis.

Even the small mouth and rock bass, who congregated in the bay a safe distance from the lure on the end of Earl's fishing line, didn't worry about my Martha. Her diet is not fish, it's grain. Rather, their concern was about Sally the seagull and her noisy gang.

I knew because I overheard a conversation last summer as I sat on the dock dangling my feet in the lake. First, all I heard was gurgling below my feet. Naturally, I yanked them out, but the gurgling continued. After putting in my hearing aid, I listened to a small mouth bass family having a deep discussion about life, Ben Johnson and seagulls' suppers.

Gertrude was giving advice to her offspring. She had, however, a secret about which she was sorely ashamed but could not bring herself to confess openly. "Let's just say," she instructed, "that you do as I say, but not as I do." Bubbles rose to the surface as she sighed with a small measure of relief.

"But, Mother, you're always telling us that we've got to be big, strong and fast like you, so that we won't become seagulls' supper. How do we do that? How did you get to be so much bigger than our aunts and uncles?"

That was her secret. "Well, fingerlings, you don't want to be too big or else you'll get caught and fried for a fisherman's feast."

"How come you're still alive, then?" they questioned. "You're bigger than big!"

"Ah, yes, but I'm strong and I'm fast, just like Ben Johnson." Ouch, she slapped herself with her shiny tail. "I shouldn't have said that!"

"Who's Ben Johnson?" Ethel asked.

"Never mind. Aye aye, me and my big mouth!"

Ethel nearly choked, "Ma, we're small mouth!"

"Never mind," she said.

"But, Mother," Eric, Ella and Ethel chorused, "we want to be just like you."

I watched as Gertrude took a flying leap right out of the water, gulped down a tiny dragonfly, then descended to join her little ones, who were lurking under the dock.

"For one thing, never eat a dragonfly – they are like darning needles. With my kind of body make-up, I can do it. You can't. Got that?"

"Uh huh," gurgled the triplets.

Ethel was desperate, "When can I start wearing make-up, Ma?"

"Ethel, please stop pestering me with questions. You're too young to wear make-up, little one. All of you, now, what did I say you have to watch out for? Ella?"

"Shiny things that swim on top of and under the water defying the laws of gravity, whatever that is, and that look like they're being towed."

"And that don't belong. Wrong colours, wrong shapes, wrong sizes," added Eric.

"Right, you two." Gertrude was proud. "What else?"

Ethel spat out, "Watch out for diving loons and if we ever do get injured, do not laze about near the surface."

"Why not?"

"We'd be seagulls' supper, for sure."

"Ya, Ma, Ethel's right. Beware of seagulls!"

As usual, Ethel was not satisfied. "Ma, stop changing the subject. Who is Ben Johnson?"

"He's a very famous Canadian who got caught for doing drugs. He won a gold medal at the Olympics for being the fastest man in the whole world in the 100-metre race, but they took his medal away from him forever. You know why?"

"Why, Ma? Tell us, please!"

"Because they found out that he had been using steroids illegally to help him run faster. He used to be my hero."

From my vantage point above, I could see the look of sadness on her face. Boy, could she pout – just like Mick Jagger.

"Jumping jellyfish, did I ever love his speed! I must admit that I've always tried to imitate him."

"You are fast, Ma," gushed the star-struck trio. "We'll never be able to keep up with you. No one can."

"Well, the main thing is . . ." Suddenly Gertrude swam away, really fast. She was having second thoughts. She knew she'd feel much better if she shared her secret, at least with her babies. Next she raced back to the dock, where she caught the three little traitors discussing her strange, big body in unflattering terms. Eric was chanting to his naïve sisters, "Ma's got a secret. Ma's got a secret. Ma's on steroids."

Right away, their mother declared, "The main thing, is that you can be smarter than I, not faster, and you can avoid becoming a fisherman's feast by constant vigilance. Me, I'm not smart, but I'm *fast*."

"What's 'vigilance'?" asked Ethel, adoringly swishing her tail against her mother's midriff.

Gertrude sighed, "Being on guard, keeping a good watch."

Staring at her mother wistfully, Ethel begged, "Oh, Ma, my watch is broken. I need a new one!"

Swimming in tight circles to rid herself of her frustration, the harried mother snapped up a water spider, not actually her favourite meal, and rallied to face her family.

As they swam in a straight line towards Gertrude, Eric and Ella boasted, "If we learn to swim as fast as you, Ma, we'll never get caught."

"That's what Ben Johnson thought, my small mouth fishies," said their wise mother.

The Great Northern Diver

The 'common' loon, I always hate that name. It sounds degrading, snobbish.

I prefer to call the loon by its original name given to him by the people who lived in community with nature, who gave us the canoe. They honoured him with the title, Great Northern Diver. The 'common' loon, therefore, will henceforth be GND (it's easier to type, for another thing!) in this article.

I'm not afraid of GNDs, but I won't swim with them. I adore them. I mean what's not to adore about a loon? Oh, I know, some say they're overrated, overexposed, elusive, and unfriendly. Actually, I read in a bird book that loons can be ferocious, especially when protecting their young or their territory. At the least, it's up to us to help them protect their young by boating slowly when close to shore.

Once, I watched in wonder what I thought was a well-choreographed mating dance performed by a pair of GNDs just outside my bay. One of their best moves involved spreading their wings and standing, yes standing, upright on the top of the water's surface! I was enthralled, and I certainly was dreaming of seeing the same two plus their babies in my bay sometime soon.

However . . .

When I read up on the fanfare and vocalization of the ritual that had mesmerized me, I learned that I'd been witnessing two males fighting – well, arguing – and jockeying for position.

Do they play games? I could swear I've seen them playing hide-and-go-seek and follow-the-leader. I've watched as one GND followed its mate or pal, dove, then came up in front of the other as if saying, "Fooled you!" Then he went behind and did exactly the same thing again. What a tease! Then they both dove, and it was all I could do to find them again when they resurfaced about ten windsurfer lengths away.

GNDs are famous for their ability to remain submerged for many, many minutes, and their unusual skill in diving to a depth of as much as 200 feet. I haven't actually timed the duration of their dives, for when you watch a pair, for instance, you can be easily fooled, or at least confused.

For proper viewing, of course, you need binoculars. I must remember to call them that instead of 'field glasses'. Mine are black, and 10 by 28, whatever that means! It does mean that in order to keep your quarry from shaking in the lens, you've got to prop your elbows on a non-moving object, such as a veranda railing. Parts of the human anatomy will not do. In the case of GNDs, however, looks are not everything.

One thing binoculars cannot do is increase volume. You're being given short shrift, I feel, if discussions of GNDs are restricted to their looks and behaviour. That just is not fair to the GND. Why not? You wouldn't ask if you'd ever *heard* a loon.

That musical magic needs to be listened to, not read about. What you'll hear are laughs, plaintive cries, sad swooning songs, screeches (not unattractive and 'common' like those of seagulls), yodels, and tremolos. You'll hear them in the evening, at night and early in the morning.

Say hello to the Great Northern Diver, and goodbye to the 'common' Loon.

For the birds

It is easy to divert me from house cleaning and bed making, when, for example, there's a conference taking place outside my bedroom window. I watched as the mother and father barn swallows took their respective perches on the bare pine branches, he a couple of feet above her. Along came a tiny, spectacular specimen, barely a fledgling, to offer objective opinions. He picked a short branch and stayed safely close to the trunk.

Now, I looked him up in my trusty bird books under thrushes and warblers, and he simply was not there. However he, a mere shadow of the real thing, did appear on the five pages devoted to sparrows. Yet the books I was using didn't do him justice on *any* of their pages. If they showed his fine bright yellow stripes under his eyes, they would leave out the dazzling one in the middle of his crown, or forget the little yellow wing bars. If I could see them then surely the ornithologist could, and the artist or photographer ought to have at least done a proper job when putting them in my books. I mean, the lovely white under parts were included, but not enough black and white speckled spotting in the upper body were shown. The closest I've come to matching my memory with a picture is that of the golden crowned sparrow.

But they don't come to Muskoka! Help! Who was he?

I think the purpose of the meeting was to decide what to do about the swallows' paranoia regarding the threatening presence of the Big Creature (me, hereafter named B.C.) inside the very house upon which the swallows had chosen for their nest. This poorly placed nest rests on the top ledge of my bedroom window. It cannot be seen from inside my room, and since the window is three body lengths above the ground there is no danger of my reaching it from the outside. I do not own an extension ladder. The chosen window is the half that cannot be moved. I will not, therefore, go after the nest from inside.

The two worriers, however, do not know this.

Every time I, the B.C., pass in front of the window or, if I as much as sit up in bed, I hear a crackling sound. At first I barely noticed it, then it penetrated my subconscious and I figured, no it's not a rattler, (I've never heard one of those though they do exist in Muskoka, and I hope I never do), not a mouse, raccoon or squirrel. It sounded like someone snapping his fingers at the speed of hummingbirds' wings. Well, by golly, when out of the corner of my eye I caught a flash of white belly with fluttering wings, I recognized the sounds' source. These frantic parents were protecting their babies from me! Now, whenever I go into that room I'm careful not to scare them.

It is very difficult taking off a wet bathing suit while in the 'stoop' position!

A nasty, not so natty, female hummingbird horned in on the meeting. The tree has never been so important – three species on one of its dead branches. Wow! Now all we need to overwhelm me is the arrival of a rose-breasted grosbeak. I know there is one around because I saw him myself. And I know I have the species right because his distinctive markings were very easy to find all on one bird in both bird books – with proper colours in all the right places.

By unanimous consent, the conference members decided on a policy of distracting the B.C. to keep her away from the poorly placed nest. And indeed, the B.C. was kept occupied by the frequent arrival of new bird species to look up in her books. She had to race down to the deck where she'd left her field glasses in order to study a flock of seagulls who had alerted her of their presence with stronger-than-usual battle cries. Next, a couple of crows cawing captured her attention, because they, standing in a menacing fashion on the bare branches of a stark dead pine, looked so much like an Edgar Alan Poe vision that she had to fetch her camera and clamber over to 'Whale Back' (the rock that juts peninsula-style into the lake.) Next, she had to wait for the sun to move a little to the side so that she wouldn't be photographing directly into it.

The hummingbirds certainly did their share of diverting the B.C.'s attention, by turning up with their families, friends and friends of friends and their in-laws, to drink from the feeder.

Thus forced the B.C. to cook and cool their syrup to refill the awkward feeder, often twice a day. Once the cooling syrup was mistakenly used in the kettle for making tea!

A great blue heron got into the act by standing on a dock far down in the bay when the B.C. was out in her canoe with her camera and rod. She didn't dare pass the heron's line of vision and so she waited and watched. As is usual with these regal birds, she was almost convinced that he was a fake, for he did not move at all. It became a duel to determine who could stay still longer. She was dying to yell to shore to tell her family about his royal presence, but was afraid he would fly away.

Well, he did, after an hour or two of serious meditation.

Frequent visits by mergansers served as marvellous diversions. The B.C. admired their baby-sitting expertise, especially when she saw the sitter in front carrying two ducklings (her own?) on her back while leading nine more in an orderly line along the shoreline. Their childish frolicking proved great entertainment.

To tell the truth, I'm not that interested in the clacking swallows anyway. It's the lone loon who visits my bay on about a weekly basis that I wait for. I wish she had a mate to cry out to, for I dearly love listening to their songs, dirges, hysterical laughs and mournful cries.

I no longer hear the swallows and I was so busy with the diversions offered that I failed to witness their flying lessons altogether. The nest, however, remains.

Will the same swallows use it next year, do you think?

Earl plays hero and rescuer

My skeptical husband didn't believe it when my cousin informed us that there had been a bear sighting on Tobin Island. He claimed that it was only the big black Newfoundland dog, which has often deceived us.

A week later, however, my cousin phoned us from Whaleback, next door to us (yikes!), to announce that they'd seen it themselves, with its brown snout, rounded ears, galloping gait and all.

Admonishing Sarah, her dog and me to stay in the main cabin and keep a good lookout for the furry creature, Earl set out to do some fishing with Laura, the daughter of our good friends a few bays to the south of us.

Meanwhile, while peering through the binoculars, I noticed that the sliding doors of the boathouse, the very same doors that lead to our kitchenette containing a jar of honey, freshly picked raspberries and all kinds of bear delicacies within, was, uh, wide open! You should have heard us making a racket with our whistles, cookie sheets and cake pans as we scrambled down the hill to secure the boathouse!

Try as we did, we never caught sight of the uninvited guest. Feeling marooned, we found reading impossible because every other word seemed to spell b-e-a-r. Suddenly I noticed a shiny, black creature at the water's edge down in Lily Bay. The binoculars revealed, however, a black rock that has been there since we bought this piece of land, and it didn't really have a bear's shape. Oh, well.

When Earl and Laura came back to switch boats for better fishing they became properly frightened. We suggested that maybe they should cruise around Norway Point just in case they might be able to spot the dangerous fellow crashing through the bush. Moments later, my cousin phoned to say the bear had just passed by her tiny cottage at Norway Point.

At this point Earl's adventure began. As he cruised towards the tip of Norway Point he pointed out to Laura, "There's something in the water near the shore." A vision of Paddington immediately flashed into his mind and he declared, "My God, it's the bear!" As he approached it, it turned to go back to shore.

Earl realized what the bear was trying to do and immediately got between him and the land, thus heading him off. The bear then proceeded to swim westwards across the lake towards the stretch of mainland between Morinus and Thorel House.

As neither Earl nor Laura was aware of the black bear's true prowess in swimming, they were both very concerned that somehow he might actually drown. This was absolutely not what they wanted. All they were trying to do was get him off Tobin Island safely on to the mainland, for he had definitely become a danger with his frequent appearances at Norway Point, which was well populated with children, adults, a couple of dogs and a cat.

Hence, they became the bear's guide, protector and escort, moving slowly behind him and waving off several boaters who were coming towards them. Other boaters' waves caused the bear to lift his head higher out of the water to keep breathing. Earl noticed that when he increased the boat's speed the bear immediately increased his. That made Earl and Laura worry that they might be putting him in danger by making him swim too fast. Maintaining enough distance between them he kept him moving towards the far shore, but at a steady, slow speed.

In awe, Laura uttered, "This is a lifetime experience." Earl readily agreed, and Sarah and I are both very jealous and mad that they had only useless fishing rods with them instead of a camera! Still worried continually that they might cause the bear to drown, they didn't know what to do. As Earl explained to Laura, "I cannot help the bear by tying a rope around his neck and towing him to shore!"

Fifteen minutes into the slow journey, a loon surfaced not more than eight feet from the bear. The loon, taking the odd dive en route, kept the bear company, swimming alongside him. Earl told me that he and Laura truly felt the loon was urging him on, telling him in its loony language, "You can make it."

They were deeply moved by this display of communication between those two black creatures of the wild.

Finally, as they got closer to land, they watched as the loon disappeared and the bear climbed up on to the shore. He stood and looked back at them, then wiggled his shiny body, shaking off the water. Next, he stretched out his forepaws, climbed further up the rocks, then quickly went out of sight into the woods.

Earl told me that he and Laura both had tears in their eyes when their black, big-headed, brown-snouted swimmer finally made it to shore after his half mile swim.

Tobin Islanders were grateful for Earl's heroics and his reputation soared.

Dawn marauder

Four-thirty in the morning was certainly not our time of choice for getting up on a Sunday morning, however our resident rust-tinted raccoon thought otherwise. While attempting to open the door of the beer fridge located at the end of a slip directly below our bedroom, he must have knocked over a couple of empties that had been resting on top. Being hard of hearing, I cannot always locate the source of sounds and therefore didn't even try. I was prepared to go straight back to sleep but my husband thought otherwise.

Two contrary souls in one morning!

In the half-light, Earl crept out to the upper deck then down the steps and, after carefully opening the boathouse door, caught sight of the marauder peering at him from his vantage point inside the fridge. Earl, growling fiercely, hastily slammed the fridge door shut, imprisoning the raccoon inside, and blocked the door. He had assumed that you scare raccoons the way you supposedly scare off bears, with sudden, sharp noises. From my safe perch on our cozy bed upstairs I couldn't tell who was making the awful jungle noises. Just to make sure that 'Rusty' knew who was boss here, Earl grabbed a paddle and banged it on the dock and the fridge.

What to do next? he pondered. He came back upstairs to discuss the situation with me. Annoyingly, I asked him, "What is he doing in *our* beer fridge?" Talented though Rusty may be, I just didn't believe he had a yen for beer and any knowhow about twist tops!

Wide awake at this point and in definite agreement with my husband regarding Rusty's future, I followed him into the lower boathouse. We decided we'd prefer an alive-yet-scared raccoon to a dead one in our fridge. Earl promptly proceeded to frighten him again by whacking the fridge with his trusty, scarred paddle.

Since it was not yet light outside, I couldn't actually see the animal as he scooted out of the fridge the moment Earl opened its door. In a flash we detected a splash as Rusty dove into the lake beside our boat.

Upon examination of his wet trail along the dock we learned how he had managed to climb up on to the side of the slip, an undertaking we had considered impossible, even for a raccoon. For him it was simple. He must have used our boat's stern ladder, then made a short leap off the boat's side onto the edge of the slip, where he left large splash spots.

What a clever fellow!

Worried about the mess we'd be faced with, we looked inside out little fridge. I was puzzled because I was certain that there was nothing there that would offer succulent scents to entice our marauder. Lo and behold, didn't my husband pull out a shopping bag and thrust it into my reluctant hands. Yuck, it was lumpy! It set my imagination on a most unattractive trail. In the dawn's early light I opened the bag and peered inside at what looked like walnut-sized black lumps.

"Horrors, oh, no!" I cried out, "Not again!" 'Twas not scat – described in the Little Oxford Dictionary as "wordless jazz song using voice as instrument, – 'twas half of our summer supply of black Moroccan olives! I had no choice: I threw them all away.

The other half rests safely inside the fridge in the main cottage where doors are always closed tight at night, and there is no convenient water access. These delectable black blobs are ready to be used in *Salade Nicoise*, *Puttanesca* and our favourite baked *fenouil au gratin aux olives noires*.

The recurring goodbye

There's almost a hush on Lake Rosseau as the end of summer approaches. While contributing to loneliness, the silence encourages meditation, and that's not such a bad thing.

Imagine my being able to sit on my deck writing a column without any distractions. Such as from Martha and her young'uns hinting for treats the way that only mallards can, vocally and with longing looks, and by positioning themselves in their favourite spot beside the boathouse. As I daydream while sitting at my little table and receive not a single visitor arriving on foot or by boat, I realize that there is no longer any justification for further procrastination. At last I find myself with pencil in hand ready to begin.

Now I can laugh about it, but several Septembers ago I was not amused. Having written what was certainly my best piece ever about the end of summer in Muskoka, I gasped when without so much as a 'How do you do?', the dastardly wind snatched my precious pile of papers, plastered with pen and ink hieroglyphics worthy of a Nobel Prize at least, and drowned them. No way could I rescue them from the clutches of such deep waters, nor was I able to recreate my Hemingway-like masterpiece, try as I did!

Indeed, there still are boats on the lake, but they're obviously also feeling the end of summer blues for they're not speeding or pulling squealing tube riders, wake boarders and water-skiers behind them. No longer flying into the bay is that little skiff with the would-be major league pitcher on board hurling *The Globe & Mail* on to our neighbour's dock. Jeepers, the lake is so unpopulated that swimming in the buff loses its label as the 'adrenaline-enhanced sport' of July and August. Today it's the colder air and water that challenge skinny dippers, who dive in covered with goose bumps and pop out with a pair of purple lips.

Proving that autumn has already begun, some maples are sporting spots of orange and red. There's one in Lily Bay, just a short one, that stands out against its background of dark, majestic evergreens. Muskoka's magical misty mornings must be mentioned as another sign of the fall's approach. On such mornings, Earl would take out *Peewee*, his little fishing punt, for a little tour in Lily Bay.

At night, the unusual darkness across the lake, excepting at Clevelands and a couple of boathouses, speaks not of menace but of peaceful slumber. When gazing upon the lake I recall the special cozy feeling I always experience in Algonquin Park late at night when my fellow campers, my three daughters, are snug in their sleeping bags inside the tent. There I feel at one with nature, safe in its embrace.

Probably writing a column for *The Muskoka Sun* is a sneaky or subconscious way for me to avoid the chores of closing up the cottage, but I cannot write non-stop. What a responsibility it is to ensure the beloved summer home will still be intact, mouse-free and without leaking pipes after winter.

The last days of summer would always have me fraught with fear that I'd leave something vital behind, something important like a computer disk, address book, or box of recipes. Earl's greatest fear, I know, was that somehow the bubblers would stop working and we'd come back to 'Shonan' and find the boathouse – with living quarters above – had taken a tumble into the lake thanks to the ice's terrible power. After all, we had lost part of one dock once, but that was before we had the boathouse and bubblers, along with someone trustworthy checking them throughout the winter.

No doubt many of you have come back to the cottage in the spring to find that the electric power or gas had not been turned off properly, or that the last of the kitchen garbage had spent the winter freezing indoors, only to start to stink up the cottage when spring thaw set in. Was a window left open, a door unlocked? Did you forget to put the toilet paper on the outhouse shelf back into its mouse-proof coffee tin? What fine nesting material that makes for mice!

Good end-of-summer-memories abound. After all our family had gone back to the city, Earl and I would brave cold, shallow waters in search of just the right pieces of driftwood. Our efforts, always amply rewarded, left us with bruised ankles, scraped toes and legs decorated up to the knees with psychedelic designs donated by underwater, spiky branches. We found many gems, including six pieces strongly resembling the letters S, H, O, N, A, and N, which we glued on a board we painted Peking red and then arranged for Larry English to secure above the front door of our four-season log cabin. It looked great!

Even in my dotage I know I'll never forget one 'last night' at the cottage. Tired and depressed, Earl, our son Jack and daughter Jessie and I went to bed early. While Earl and I were lying in our bed a strange sound stirred our hearts, not with fear but with anticipation. What the heck was this? It was getting louder and coming closer. We got up to look down at the black lake, for there were neither stars nor moon on this melancholy night, and detected (we thought) the outline of a long launch cruising into our bay. We recognized the musical sound as being someone's laughter. It was enchanting, but the best was yet to come.

After waking Jack and Jessie up, we grabbed flashlights and headed down to the lake. No, we weren't frightened because the laughter dispelled such notions. Besides, it was contagious, and became more so when we realized it was coming from our lively cousin Carmen. A deep, sober voice boomed as the boat drifted a few meters beyond the end of our dock. The boat came to a stop when the engine quit and a splash announced the dropping of an anchor.

"Ahoy, landlubbers!" Terry hollered, as more voices echoed the same words with lovely Argentinean and Brazilian accents. The skipper, our first cousin once removed, shone his floodlight over the cast of costumed characters striking outlandish poses aboard the rocking stage.

On board were: a very tall fellow dressed in drag; hip swaying, provocative female dancers, some holding a faded boa; saluting soldiers in WWI uniforms; a hobo leaning on the crutch made out of a tree branch for my father to use while recovering from his war wounds; and a few bathing-suit-clad sopranos, tenors, altos and baritones serenading us with South American songs (I think).

They thought they were terribly funny, and so did we. Always Carmen's tinkling laughter provided the background music as we stared dumbfounded at the rakish group exhibiting hilarious poses. Obviously both the wine and the costume trunk had been opened. Wow, what a sight! That was the best farewell we ever experienced at 'Shonan', although midnight paddles in the moonlight on the quiet lake, and bonfires at Canoe Rock with singing and storytelling come a close second and third.

While it seems as though this column has reached its nostalgic conclusion, it has not. Bear with me briefly, there is just one more summer sound that must be praised, for it has always welcomed me back to the city from Muskoka. I hear it tonight in all its splendour and it lifts my heart – a chorus of cheerful chirping crickets.

The little sock

It was a crisp autumn evening in Pierrefonds, with pale orange pine needles flitting like snow past Grace's study windows. Although her windows were closed, her concentration was interrupted by the sound of the wind as it shook brown, yellow and scarlet leaves, rustling violently against the wind's onslaught. Gazing through her west-facing window, she was struck by the sight etched by the sun during its descent, peering through occasional clouds and enfolding one orange-leafed maple tree in its golden shroud. It turned the maple into a picture frame for the skyscrapering evergreen that stood between her and the highlighted maple, looking like a stencil.

Unfortunately, the sun beat her to it and disappeared as Grace galloped downstairs to fetch her camera. "Oh, that would have been a wonderful photograph!" she complained, while catching her breath at the front door.

"Are you talking to me?"

"No, Earl, I'm just frustrated."

"What's the matter, Gracie? Can I help?"

Turning back into the house, she explained, "No, this is certainly one thing you can't help with unless you can don some wings and fly to the sun, throw a lasso around it and haul it back up into sight." With a feeling of relief she smiled, "Mm, that would make a good picture, too!" The look on Earl's face, so puzzled yet willing, made her laugh. "It's okay, Earl, I haven't lost my marbles, but you look so, well, so . . ." – she wasn't going to say endearing; that'd be going too far – "ah, eager. I feel a bit better now."

Earl put his hands on her shoulders and guided her to her favourite chair in the living room. "I'm glad you're feeling better, dear, but I'm still confused. What's this about wings?"

With a snort she uttered, "Forget it, it's too hard to explain. It's my own fault: I shouldn't let myself get so upset all the time. Lord, why am I so sensitive these days anyway?"

Earl burst out laughing, "Don't tell me that you, my seventy-five year old wife, are actually pregnant?"

"Oh, you rascal! By gum, I'd rather be pregnant than the way I am these days. I've been so emotional!"

"Haven't you noticed, my dear, I haven't exactly been up to snuff either?"

After blowing her nose, Grace looked at her husband, "I've been far too wrapped up in myself to notice, Earl, that's the truth." Suddenly she leaped up and headed for the kitchen, "I'll make us a couple of tea and we can talk. We're in this together and I know we must move on."

The soothing sound of water running from the kitchen tap and the banging of the kettle's lid had a calming effect on them both. A couple of tea was just the ticket, as Grace would often say. Earl fetched a tray and placed the cups, saucers, sugar bowl, and a carton of milk on it, then carried it through to the living room. Grace followed soon after with the heavy Brown Betty teapot.

Sitting side by side on the sofa they stirred their tea while waiting for it to cool, since they each had added only a drop of milk to it. Earl commented: "This is certainly not like the NAAFI tea I drank in England at the end of the war."

"You mean white tea?" An ugly grimace changed her gentle looks completely, "I never liked that stuff. Ugh!"

"I know, dear. The tea was so strong you had to dilute it with a lot of milk, or cream if you were lucky. In fact, that's how it was served to you, already mixed, unless you asked for black tea."

"Having tea in Lyons Corner Houses always made me feel very English. I guess you could compare the Corner Houses to Murray's – decent food and prices. Know what I did when I came back from my post-grad year in England? I developed the habit of adding Lapsang Souchong to the teapot." While pouring their second cups she started to giggle, "Liv always says it smells like leather when I add it!"

"Well, it does. Gracie. Are you feeling better now? For good I mean?"

"Yes, dear. I'm just getting used to the idea of not having the cottage any more. What a wrench it's been! I do miss it so much. But I know we did the right thing and the children are also getting on with their lives, planning different kinds of vacations and such."

"As are we," interrupted Earl with enthusiasm. "We have much to look forward to, and you have to admit the seven-hour drive was becoming quite tiring."

"And look at the price of gas! Oh, Earl, I do love this house and it is fun fixing it up, isn't it?" She chuckled, "We really did neglect this place over the years. Oh, I can't wait to get started with spring planting next year."

A happy voiced announced, "And I cannot wait to have my own vegetable garden!"

Patting her husband's knees, Grace promised, "No more blue moods. I think today was getting me down especially because it's our first Thanksgiving away from the cottage in twenty-two years. I know it's hard on the kids, too, but we'll convert the basement into a comfy place for all the grandchildren to play in and I'll bake all their favourite things, and we've already replaced some of the old beds and mattresses with new ones. Next year we'll get them all here for Thanksgiving. We'll feast, go for nature walks, look at photo albums together. You and the boys can talk about cars, and the girls and I will reminisce about their childhood and our all-girl camping trips in Algonquin Park. They can see their old friends, too."

"We have to be careful, dear. We mustn't forget that they have their own lives to lead, their own families and in-laws," he sighed. "But you have me looking forward to next Thanksgiving already and the gardening, redecorating – thanks Grace, I'm glad we finally talked about this." Another sigh escaped as he covered his mouth.

"There's nothing a couple of tea can't fix."

While Earl was leaving the living room carrying the tea tray, the telephone rang.

"I'll get it in my study, Earl." She picked up the telephone. Tears welled up in her eyes as she listened to their forty-three-year-old son explaining between sobs that he had finally unpacked his last box of belongings and souvenirs from the cottage. He told her he'd been doing just fine about selling the cottage until today, when he went and opened up and found the contents in the last one.

"Oh, Matt, I know how you feel. Those boxes contained twenty-two years of memories, don't I know it!"

Miserably, she flopped down on a chair to listen. "Of course I understand. It's sad for us all. In fact, your dad and I have just finished discussing this very thing and somehow we think we've managed to overcome our sorrow and – just a second," she grabbed a tissue and blew her nose, "we're now ready to take the next steps together. Let me get this right. It was the little sock that set you off?"

Tears flowed anew down Grace's cheeks. "Dad and I couldn't throw it away. Of course you fell apart completely when you found it nestled in your favourite Muskoka mug! I would have, too. I suggest you frame it and protect it behind glass and put it up on the wall and take a photo of it to give to your son for Christmas, even if it does make him cry. In fact, Matt, could you send us a photo of it, too? After all, Lon is our first grandchild."

"I know. Lon may be twenty-three now, but from age one on he spent every summer up there. I agree with you, this is probably harder on him than on any of us. Poor kid!"

162

Relieved that Matt's voice was becoming stronger, she asked him, "Do you know the story of Lon's little sock?"

Overhearing Grace's one-sided conversation with their son, Earl quietly slipped into her study and stood behind her, folding his arms around her shoulders. She reached up to clutch his hand.

"Now, don't make me cry again!" She shuddered. "Isn't that the cutest little sock you've ever seen? I can picture it now, tacked up on the wall near the wood stove in our beautiful cottage for all to see. Considering that two-inch beige, white and brown striped sock spent a whole winter lying unprotected on the ground in Muskoka near the steps to the cottage, it's amazing it didn't simply disintegrate when I picked it up in May. It must be a cotton-polyester mix. Heck, Matt, it feels like only yesterday when I found it lying on a pile of dead pine needles and oak leaves. It smelled marvellous, almost like lichens – you know, that 'good earth' smell."

"It still has that Muskoka smell? Guard it with your life, Matt!"

Part 3

Everyday Tea:
Habits, rituals
and daily life

The best gift

Settling in back home in their city house after four months at the cottage took no time, for they were used to it. They always found, however, that at first they'd have to search for things like the garlic press and sugar bowl, and try to remember which cupboard had the dish towels in it, for instance. The biggest adjustment was having to turn off the toaster oven after each use because the one at the cottage shut off automatically whenever anyone opened its door.

The first morning back they sat at their kitchen table enjoying a breakfast of bacon and eggs plus toast and their couple of tea. They always allowed themselves a cooked breakfast on their first morning back home. After that day, breakfasts were ordinary.

How they loved their little routines! And yet this fall something was not right. Whenever Grace sat at the kitchen table and looked out the front window she had the oddest feeling. Something was missing, but what? Finally she expressed her worry to Earl. It was a Monday morning when she blurted, "Earl, it's already 8:15. Something is missing!"

"You're forgetting, Gracie, that clock is always twenty minutes fast."

"Not any more, dear."

Looking fondly up at the old clock he noticed the small sign attached to it stating in capital letters, 'This clock is on time'. Originally it had been Grace's idea to set it ahead in order to facilitate getting the children off to school on time. A smile creased his face as he reminisced. "Uh, sorry, dear, what's missing?"

"Oh, I don't know. But I do know that this place is not the same as it was when we left in June."

With a shrug, he said, "Of course it isn't. It was spring then and now it's fall. It's chillier and the cedars are not as green; that's all."

"No, it's not that."

"Do you think we were robbed, you mean?" He gave another shrug. "I haven't noticed anything. It would help, dear," and he smiled patronizingly, "if you knew what was taken." Picking up the newspaper he continued reading about the latest political scandals involving the Federal Government.

Hurriedly Grace took her sports section, tea and toast to the dining room and called out, "Don't you think I'd tell you if I knew what it was!" In her exasperation she slammed her cup down so hard that one third of its contents lurched in a tidal wave over the tablemat. "Darn, see what you made me do!"

"I'm sorry. I'm sorry, Grace. You're upset!" Earl came running to her with a dripping dishrag. "Here, I'll clean this up, dear, and I'll make you a fresh cup." He bent down and planted a peck on the top of her head.

"Thanks, dear. I know I'm acting silly, but I've had this feeling ever since we got home, and I'd been so looking forward to our morning ritual complete with the newspaper. I do so miss the newspaper in Muskoka. Maybe we should get it delivered to us."

"Agreed, dear, but you're the one who prefers *The Gazette* to *The Globe and Mail*. Can't you just see our Quebec paper being delivered to our island?"

"It might get tossed into the lake instead of on the dock." Mustering a smile, she returned to the kitchen with her cup and newspaper section while Earl, having put a new tea bag into the Brown Betty teapot and poured boiling water over it, bought it to the table and asked nervously, "All set?"

"Yes, thanks, Earl. Whatever is bothering me I can't imagine." She resumed reading, for the hundredth time, about this being the final year of the Expos in Montreal. "I wish the Expos didn't have to go! Heavens to Betsy, they'd better not do that to the Canadiens. I couldn't survive without watching 'my Glorieux'!"

"I agree, the Expos have certainly given us entertainment, even if they haven't ever made it all the way to the World Series."

"They would if they didn't have all those fire sales!"

"True, true," uttered Earl, paying more attention to an article about the benefits of eating Nutella. Obviously, since he was known as Mr. Nutella among their friends because he spread it on his toast every single day for breakfast, the article was pleasing him immensely. "Gracie, have you heard how they pronounce Nutella in the television ads?"

"The same way everybody does, Nutella, of course."

"No, you're wrong. They pronounce the nut to rhyme with puke, and that makes me feel like puking."

"Earl, for the luvva Mike, you're dizzgusting – as Mum would say!"

Not looking remotely contrite, Earl rubbed salt into the wound, "Oh, dear, did I spoil your breakfast?"

"And how! And if you don't control yourself immediately I'll – guess what I'll do, it almost rhymes with that horrible word you used – yes 'shoot' you with this." She raised her cup of tea.

"Sorry, my love, I went too far."

"Yes, you did. Now pour us another couple of tea. There's a dear."

A few mornings later Grace observed her husband gazing abstractedly off in the distance through the kitchen window. "A penny for your thoughts?" she prodded.

"No thoughts. I'm sort of waiting. Oh, I don't know, looking for something, I guess."

"For what? Now you're being as vague as I was the other day."

"And like you said, if I knew the answer to that I'd tell you, Grace."

Looking at the clock – now minus its little notice, the result of her husband's tinkering – Grace became animated. "It's 8:20. Oh, Earl, I know what it is! Where are our little Haitian girls?

This is the time they always walk by on their way to catch their bus."

"Is it 8:15?"

"No, you weren't listening. It's 8:20 and they always pass by at this time every single week day. So that's what we've been missing – our two little Haitian girls."

"You are right, Gracie. I'm glad you figured it out! It's strange. I wonder why we haven't seen them. I'm sure I'd have noticed if they were out there waving and smiling and running to catch their bus."

"Do you think they've changed bus stops? Or maybe they've changed schools, or – heaven forbid – moved!"

Standing up, Earl shouted, "I hope not! I do so love their bright smiles and frantic waving." Looking a bit embarrassed, he confessed, "They make me feel young again, the way we were when our kids were going off to elementary school. Those smiles jump-start my day."

"I couldn't agree with you more, dear." Chuckling, she added, "They're always in such a hurry. Of course, they're always late and the older one has such a hard time getting the little one to keep going. One day they'll miss their bus, I'm sure."

"Have you forgotten, my dear, they did."

The excited pair lingered over breakfast talking about their girls – they didn't know their names – and how important their greetings had become to them. They went over Earl's quandary on that snowy, January morning when Grace had already left in her car to do a spot of grocery shopping in case the roads would be closed later on. Earl reminisced, "That's right, you left the house at about 8 and I left soon after you to get gas, and I saw

171

two forlorn looking girls shivering violently at their bus stop. I guess it was after 8:30 and I figured they'd been playing in the snow and maybe even spent time trying to get our attention at the window when we weren't even sitting there. Anyway, they must've missed their bus. I even thought maybe because of the storm their school bus hadn't come at all. What was I to do?"

Tut-tutting while Earl talked, Grace listened attentively. She loved this tale of Earl's heroics, if you could call them that. "Well, you did the right thing, Earl. I'm proud of you."

"But it was so hard to do! I was stuck between a rock and a hard place. I was afraid to leave them there in the cold, but I also didn't dare bring them into my car even though that's what they desperately needed. Anyway I called out to them that I'd go home and find out if the buses were running late or if they were running at all. The older one – she'd be eight or so?"

"I guess so, and the little one must be about six."

"The little one wasn't too miserable playing in the snow, but the older one was crying." He shuddered, "I felt so bad leaving them out there, but I knew I couldn't pick them up. Someone, no doubt, would accuse me of being a dirty old man!"

Grace banged her hand on the table, "I know. Isn't it awful that you had to think about that? What's the world coming to?"

"It's a good thing I had my cellphone and was able to get hold of Marion. She knows everybody, where they live, who's having a baby, who's sick, and a lot more, I suppose."

"I know. She's a good neighbour, interested in everybody."

"Well, she was wonderful, let me tell you. Both helpful and very concerned." Earl rubbed his hands together, remembering his adventure.

"She's very kind, I know. Luckily she knew where the girls' sitter lived."

Earl added, "More than that, she offered to phone the woman and suggest that I come and pick her up in the car to take her to the kids. I love stories with happy endings. I wonder what's happened to them."

"Tell you what, why don't we take our walk early and go looking for them this morning?" she suggested. "What do you think? You go along Chestnut, Poplar and around that way and I'll go the opposite way to cover more territory. We'll do it tomorrow and the next day taking different routes. Okay?"

"We'll need to stay out there about an hour, in case their time has changed, too."

Happy that they would be doing at least something about their missing girls, Grace went back to reading her paper.

After a while she added, "If we don't find them I bet Marion can tell us what's happened to them."

"Come on, Gracie, we don't want Marion thinking we've fallen off our rockers just because we're missing the friendly greetings of those two little girls."

"It's not that we're off our rockers, Earl, it's just that our girls always get our day started on the right foot, so to speak. They make me feel needed again."

"Don't get me wrong, sweetheart. I feel the same as you do."

"Like Jim, our beloved bus driver," Grace teased. Changing the subject, she announced, "Well, I have good news for you, dear. All the kids are coming home for Christmas. I think September 11th has done that to a lot of families. They want to celebrate together."

"You are probably right, Grace. Are Jessie and Ben really coming? It will be such a long drive for them with a lively nine-month-old baby. It's at least six hours from St. Catharines."

"Yes, they are coming. Travis will probably sleep most of the way."

With a chuckle Earl added, "And stay awake all night!"

"Earl! Liv and Rick and the three boys are coming and that's a much worse drive especially as they have to go through Algonquin Park, where there are no gas stations or stores or motels."

"And no towers for cellphones, either. It will take them at least seven hours from Bracebridge with comfort and gas stops, but I am very glad they are coming this year. It's been a long time since they've been able to do it. At least it won't be as difficult for Jack, although you often meet snow around Kingston. I'm glad he chose Toronto instead of Halifax!"

"I can't wait till Christmas!"

"That reminds me: I have work to do. I'll start putting up the outdoor lights next week. Do we have any spare bulbs?" Earl stood up to clear his dishes, then stood there rubbing his hands together. Watching him gave Grace great pleasure.

She planned to ensure that the family visit would have a real Quebec ambience. "I want the grandchildren to see where their parents come from, you know. We'll take them to the Lookout, to see Ogilvy's wonderful window display with its old-fashioned scene, and if it isn't too cold we can have a ride in a *calèche*. We'll all go skating at Beaver Lake on Boxing Day like we used to do."

"Speak for yourself, dear. I don't think my 75-year-old legs are up to it."

"Nor mine, even if they are two years younger than yours. Ugh!" She groaned as she caught sight of the ugly veins creeping down her legs.

When they went for their walk the next morning, they searched and searched for their Haitian girls, but to no avail. After three days of trying, they stayed outside to finish stringing up the lights. Suddenly Grace got a brainwave. "Earl, look at that spruce! It's practically touching the ground. Boy, has it grown! Anyway don't you think we ought to cut off the lower branches so we can get a better view of the street from the kitchen window? Maybe the girls can't see us, or we can't see them!"

"Good thinking, dear. Last year I certainly noticed that they had to bend down to catch our attention with their frantic waving. Perhaps they can't be bothered anymore."

Clutching at straws was what they were doing, she realized. They spent the whole afternoon taking off a few branches then sawing them into four-foot lengths, tying them into bundles and piling them neatly at the curb for the next garbage collection.

Feeling elated when she went in for their tea, Grace pointed out how much lighter it was in the kitchen. "I know you don't like it when I get a brainwave, but this one was a good one; admit it."

"If it means we get to see the girls, it was," came Earl's cheerful reply. Suddenly his eyebrows knitted into a frown as he declared, "We'll be sitting like goldfish in a fish bowl from now on."

"Why goldfish? Oh, I get it, you meant because we're golden-agers. Don't worry, dear, I promise not to lick my plate." They both laughed.

Stroking his chin and leaning towards Grace, he rubbed it against her cheek and asked, "Does this mean I have to shave every day?"

"Of course, dear, there was method in my madness." Another bout of laughter ensued.

"In that case, you'd better go out and buy yourself a new robe, old girl. Honestly, that one you wear is ready for the rag box, I swear!"

Emitting a snort, Grace muttered, "More method in my madness, dear boy. We'll call it an early Christmas present from you."

"I'll order a big prime rib roast from Le Biftek for Christmas Eve. I think that is one of my favourite Christmas traditions," Earl confessed. "I'll call it an early Christmas present from you!"

"You look after the roast, Earl, and I'll pick up a nice, big frozen turkey. By the way, if you dread carving the roast we can get Matt to do it – he's good at it. Let me see; I'll get Jack to make the gravy, he's done it before."

"Oh, no you don't! I get a fancy roast of beef once a year and I'm not letting anyone touch it with that electric knife you bought! No one gets the slices thin enough for me. He can carve the turkey, though."

"Good, I'm glad that's settled."

The little girls never came but winter did, with a vengeance. Cleaning the front walk kept them busy and fit. Lit up with midnight blue lights around its front windows and along the top rail of the fence beside it, the house looked cozy and very welcoming. The excited couple had built up a high snow bank parallel to the driveway, ending in the deep ditch that would be perfect for tobogganing. Inside the house, the living and dining rooms were decorated with pine sprigs, Christmas cards attached to dangling ribbons and a bay window shelf covered with fake snow and sleds, little people, little trees, squirrels, deer, rabbits and a bright red cardinal perched on the roof of a snow-spattered log cabin. The highlight was a clay model of Santa sitting in a wooden sleigh.

The Christmas tree was up and waiting for the arrival of the children and grandchildren. Grace and Earl had put some of the decorations on it leaving some of the children's favourites for them to hang themselves.

Reaching out from his father's arms, Keegan, the youngest grandchild, would be placing the angel at the top this year. Each grandchild had a bauble with his own name on it to hook on to the lowest branches.

The biggest snowfall of the decade began late on December 23rd and continued steadily through most of the 24th. "Oh, dear," cried Grace, "I don't want the children driving in this!"

"Don't worry, the Department of Highways would close the roads if they weren't safe, dear."

It was lunchtime and they were sitting down for a light meal since they knew they'd be feasting on the famous roast beef plus other favourites followed by Earl's divine Christmas log that night. The phone's ringing interrupted the heavy quiet.

"I'll get it," Earl declared rushing to the hallway. With a forlorn look on his face he returned to tell her, "Looks like you got your wish, my love. That was Sarah to tell us that she'd spoken to her brothers and sisters, and they've agreed to postpone their travelling to tomorrow."

"You mean they're not coming until Christmas day? In a way I'm relieved," she conceded through quivering lips. "Oh, dear, that means we have to skip Christmas Eve. Shoot, tonight is just as important as Christmas day! What'll we do? We've got such a lovely dinner planned and they have to hang up all their stockings and, and . . ." Poor Grace grabbed her napkin to wipe away her tears.

Equally disappointed, Earl offered, "We'll not skip Christmas Eve. We'll move it to the 25th and celebrate Christmas on the 26th."

"You're crazy, Earl. This is Christmas Eve. What will you and I do tonight?"

"Leave it all to me. I'll make a nice dinner for us, something simple, and we'll open that special wine your cousin brought us from France to go along with it." Rubbing his hands together, he added, "It would be wasted on the kids anyway. They don't like red wine."

Giving him a big hug, she sputtered, "You are an angel. I love your idea and so will the kids."

"You can call it a bonus, in a way. It's as though we've been given an extra day in our lives."

"You're right," Grace nodded. "You've cheered me up already."

After eating one of Earl's specialties, hot dogs, salad and chips, Grace curled up on the sofa with her book. Earl had started the fire and poured them each a brandy. He noticed that while she was looking at her book, she wasn't turning the pages and, finding it hard himself to concentrate on his book, he understood.

Startling them both, the doorbell sounded.

Grace dropped her book on the floor, "Who could that be at this hour?"

Headed for the door, Earl pointed out that it was only 8 o'clock. "I expect it's some carollers."

"No, it's them, they've come after all! Outa-my-way, Earl, you big lug. It's the kids!"

"Slow down, woman, it can't be. Okay, go ahead, open the door."

Looking through the tiny glass spy-hole and seeing nothing, she opened the door with a jerk. There stood two smiling black-eyed, black-haired girls bundled in red snowsuits. Peering over his wife's shoulder, Earl declared, "Wonderful, wonderful! I'd recognize those smiles anywhere! Girls, please come in. Gracie, where are your manners?"

"Oh, girls, where have you been? We've been looking for you since November! Have you moved?" She asked, bending down to talk to them.

The older girl explained that they had changed schools and were getting a lift to school from their mother on her way to work. "Your house looks different. What happened to your big tree?" She asked shyly.

"We cut the lower branches off it," Earl replied.

Stepping forward, the younger girl handed Grace a large paper bag with string handles and then said, "Merry Christmas."

Giving them both big hugs, Grace declared, "Oh, girls, this is the best gift ever!"

"It certainly is!" agreed Earl, rubbing his hands together.

Giggling, the older girl asked, "How can you tell, you haven't opened it yet."

Earl explained that seeing them was the best gift. "Thank you for coming. We've missed you both so much."

Smiling again, the older girl spoke to her sister, "We have to go now, Celie. Mama is waiting for us." Arm in arm, Grace and Earl watched as the two figures disappeared up the street.

Now they had a perfect centrepiece for their dining room table, a scarlet poinsettia. But the best gift of all was seeing the smiles on the faces of their two young friends lighting up the snowy night as they wished them "Merry Christmas."

My favourite winter activity

The driveway needs clearing. Out I go.

The bigger the snowstorm, the more I like it. When I'm shovelling snow I can't be washing floors, peeling potatoes, making beds, writing the cheques to pay the bills, stirring a white sauce non-stop without allowing a single lump and never leaving it even if the phone rings. No, when I'm shovelling snow I'm in my own white world, comfortably encased in warm clothes and feeling peacefully alone out there.

When snow is falling, all outdoor sounds are muffled. Off in the distance there might be a snowplough operating but it doesn't bother me – it's just good company, the kind that makes its presence known but doesn't intrude. And maybe from time to time I'll hear an engine racing and wheels spinning, typical city or suburban winter sounds. Now and then I'll also hear a snow shovel scraping ice or bare pavement . . . lovely.

Boy, do I love winter!

The birds are silent. They're busy snuggling inside the cedar hedge that borders my property. It gives them the warmth and cover they cherish. Sometimes when it's not so cold I hear constant chatter coming from my hedge. But . . . not today. Now the snowing has stopped and the temperature has dropped to minus 12, but the sun is shining. It's the kind of stark cold that causes airplanes overhead to sound as though they're coming in for a landing in my own yard! As my eyes rove, I catch hints of blue in the snow – such a magic, elusive sight.

I figure I have at least an hour's work ahead to clear my driveway. The city plough hasn't come yet, but if it does, I can add another half hour. Good. I love being out here. I've developed an easy rhythm. It goes like this: thrust, lift, then swing my body sideways and bend the knees, toss behind me. I have a bad back, so I have to do it that way rather than throwing the snow in front or to the side where I can see where it's going. Being used to my snow-shovelling stance, I know exactly what force to use to pitch. The load always lands off the driveway.

Anyway, most Canadians know the mechanics of clearing fresh snow from driveways and sidewalks. That is the part that makes the body feel alive and healthy. The more I shovel, the more energy I have.

Does that happen to you?

The mechanics, however, are not really the important part of the process, not for me anyway. Because I crave the freedom and sense of power and control I get from working in cold air in a quiet, pristine world, I actually prefer to do the job alone. This is not a chore – it is my all-time favourite form of winter activity. When I'm thrusting, lifting, swinging, bending, and tossing I'm actually fulfilling my dreams, writing new stories, planning fabulous meals for gourmet dinners, or creating and organizing and succeeding in a business venture and then spending the excessive profits.

One such business, which I named 'Cooks' Night Out', had me owning a beautifully equipped van whose insides resembled a luxury airplane's galley (but were bigger and better). There were also gorgeous dishes and attractive cutlery, along with Provence-style serving dishes and tablecloths and napkins. Add to this my hiring of my whole family to do the cooking, marketing, shopping, delivering, serving, and graphics for the menus, bills, and sides of the van and uniforms. The uniforms varied according to the theme of the meal, be it Italian, Creole, Mexican, Canadian, French, German, Tunisian, Indian, Chinese, Greek, Californian, or Spanish. Of course, for this thriving enterprise I had fantastic ovens of all kinds, and dishwashers, knives, peelers, different shaped baking pans, cutting boards, spices galore, and pots with fresh herbs sprouting out of them!

The more the snow, the longer the list of supplies.

How to spend the profits? Let me see, it's a bit like buying a lottery ticket. Some of the cash goes to my favourite charities, some to my children, some to get my husband his dream car and maybe a new boat and give him another trip to Australia. It will also go to season theatre tickets and tickets for the many great shows that come to Toronto, like 'The Phantom of the Opera' and 'Show Boat'. I wish I had seen 'Joseph and the Technicolor Dreamcoat' when Donnie Osmond was starring in it in Toronto.

Choosing charities and foundations and opportunities for education I'd like to initiate keeps me going at least another half-hour.

In a lighter vein, I've had fun playing in movies with some of my favourite actors such as Anthony Hopkins, Jack Lemmon, Oskar Werner, Yves Montand, Ingrid Bergman, Patricia Neal, Simone Signoret, and Geraldine Page. You can't begin to imagine the inspiring conversations I've had with Pierre Trudeau, Barbara Frum, Margaret Laurence, and Nelson Mandela. And the words I've had with Winnie Mandela!

Are you frustrated? Upset? Well there is no better way to air your frustration and let go of your anger than with a great heave of a shovel full of heavy snow. It is hugely satisfying. It works even better if you add vocal accompaniment as you flex your muscles. How about, "Take that, Mr. Parizeau!" or "Why wash these dishes, they're just going to get dirty again!"

Oh, dear, when I think of frustration or anger, I work much too fast. Heck, I've finished the whole dang driveway already in less than an hour! But, hark, what is that clanging, jangling sound I hear? Aha! It's the snowplough and it's on my street. Joyfully, I await a huge pile at the bottom of my cleared driveway. The plough operator certainly doesn't disappoint me. He's really reliable – he always widens the street all the way to the grass and shoves his 'pickings' all across the driveway.

Half an hour later my body is crying for a change of activity. I go into the house, shed boots, mitts and jacket and head straight for the kitchen. I don't need big muscles or effort to make a smooth, white sauce. Steadily stirring butter, flour and milk or cream is therapeutic. Like shovelling snow!

Earl's Log

Be prepared; Christmas is coming. In mid-November it's time to stock up on things like eggs, good unsalted (sweet) butter and chocolate Chipits. Unfortunately, our Costco doesn't always have the Chipits in stock. You have to grab them when you can, even as early as September. That has its drawbacks, though, because when baking time rolls around half your supply has disappeared, gone towards the spare tire I'm sporting neatly hidden by my very blouson-style tops.

Also, unfortunately, no one around here stocks the right butter at the right price, thus necessitating a quick trip to Ottawa's Costco to purchase the stuff. Don't tell *me* that the cost of gas has already made that butter more expensive than Metro's or Provigo's, tell *Earl*!

Furthermore, since the bargain eggs sold at Costco are extra large, we're not really getting top egg value for our money. They say the best eggs for baking are the medium – something to do with the ratio of yolk to white, I think. Tell *that* to my husband!

He is getting ready to make his famous 'Yule log' (or *Buche de Noel* to make it sound more exotic) for ourselves and friends. This is his greatest culinary achievement, we all agree. But the lucky recipients outside this house have no idea of the blood, sweat, swearing, tantrums, smashed spatulas, burnt wax paper, and clogged Mixmaster joints that the log produces. And that's saying nothing of the four to six dozen egg whites taking up space in my fridge until I buy sufficient sugar with which to make the meringues to avoid wasting the whites.

Never mind if the sticky meringues more than replace the saving – in dental bills!

Originally Earl used wax paper on the baking sheets for the sponge-jelly-roll part. Not even once did this part work out the way it is described in the cookbook.

Usually, before the middle was cooked the edges were already curling up with the browning wax paper stuck on it. Then my despairing husband would get us to wrap and roll the cake, paper and all in clean, damp dish towels to soften it and 'ease' the removal of the wax paper.

Try as he might, a hotter oven, cooler oven, a higher shelf, lower shelf, buttered wax paper, oiled wax paper – nothing worked. Then along came PAM and now, bravo, the cake comes off the sheet absolutely beautifully, ready to roll around the filling. I dare not suggest it, but it's my guess that parchment paper would also work, if it is available.

Now that he has perfected his technique after years of hardship, I can't eat the stuff since it's loaded with egg yolk and real butter and my poor arteries greedily grab all that cholesterol!

It is the chocolate filling that used to clog the Mixmaster, because Earl would triple the recipe so he wouldn't have to spend more than two weeks cooking and cursing every evening after work making his log supply. Often it would simply be too thick or too sugary to spread. Now he knows you cannot triple recipes, especially those containing eggs – the wrong sized ones at that!

The advent of the non-stick vegetable spray has changed all our lives for the better. Now it's 'a piece of cake' for Earl to make the cake part. You can be sure that PAM, or any other such spray, is on top of his shopping list.

The log has become a favourite Christmas tradition with family and friends alike. No wonder!

Not the way I heard it

It's all very well having an active imagination, but it can get you into trouble and waste a lot of time. I ought to know.

Once upon a time when Sarah and I were carrying on an enlightened conversation while walking her two little schnauzers, we stopped to admire a lovely garden. Sarah informed me, "The lady who lives here loves to read. I see her reading all the time when I walk the dogs."

My mind was already working overtime as I pictured a lady, with book in hand, sitting on her veranda steps. I was even pondering what books she read when Sarah interrupted the flow of my thoughts with:

"She even reads in other people's gardens."

Wow, I immediately envisioned the lady lugging her lawn chair up the street to sit on someone else's lawn, perhaps under a shady tree of which none existed on her own front lawn. Maybe she borrowed the owners' chair for this purpose, if there was one handy. Honestly, I was a bit surprised by this presumptuous behaviour, but then I knew, of course, that readers tend to be different, liberal and resourceful, you could say.

Meanwhile, while I was conjuring up this amazing picture of a real reader, my facial expression prompted Sarah to ask, "What's the matter?"

"Boy, she has a lot of nerve, doesn't she?"

"Actually, Mum, her neighbours appreciate what she does. More than once I've heard them thanking her."

"Thanking her?"

Sarah continued, "Well, Mum, wouldn't you like it if your neighbour wanted to weed your lawn?"

That afternoon when we were indulging in a cup of tea in her living room the dogs suddenly started barking. They continued for a couple of minutes then settled down again.

"They always bark at the drunk male," Sarah explained.

At once I envisioned an inebriated man weaving up her street and stumbling on to her lawn before continuing on his merry way. I was amused that my daughter had used the word male rather than man but figured the poor guy had the nickname on her street as 'the drunk male'. As I was leaving her house she, pointing at the pile of junk mail that had been pushed through her letterbox, complained, "See what I mean?"

"Oh!" I said, and laughed, leaving poor Sarah quite puzzled.

Those incidents with Sarah brought to mind some other times when I heard incorrectly. Hearing in rhyme actually promoted my imagination and gave my brain a good workout. My audioprothesist explained that it is a common ailment, the failure to identify consonants.

Accents are another problem. One time when we were living in England, I spent a frustrating afternoon watching a soccer game while sitting beside the father of the English team's star player. All our remarks to one another were extremely polite (you know the English) yet distinctly odd. When I told my husband, who was sitting on my other side, about the weird conversation, he could not stop laughing. Finally, he told me about my mistake. Well, I couldn't get away fast enough for I knew I must have seemed a real idiot to that polite parent. You see, I thought he was discussing ailments with his *spine*. I figured the subject came up because he'd injured it in a soccer match.

There I'd been tut-tutting and making sympathetic remarks to the gentleman when, in fact, he'd been telling me all about a trip to *Spain*. Jeepers, he'd used the words "trip" and "spine" in the same sentence, hadn't he?

Back in Canada, when Earl and I invited Dot and Ted over for lunch, we got into a discussion about allergies. I told them about the comfort of having an Epi-Pen at home in case someone experienced anaphylactic shock. I – showing off, no doubt – explained that our guests could always look after themselves if necessary by not eating peanuts or its derivatives, however it would not be so easy for us to avoid their being stung by a bee, if that was the cause of their particular allergy.

This was serious stuff we were discussing.

To my surprise, I heard Earl tell Dot, "My son reacted from eating a pear yesterday."

Big deal, why would he bring our son's minor allergy into this life-and-death topic? I couldn't stop myself from reacting, "Matt's not allergic to fruit!"

Well, Earl straightened me out in a hurry with, "I said *tongue*, not *son*!"

Quick as a whip, I retorted, "That's not the way I heard it."

That statement was to be repeated many times in my life.

As soon as Dot and Ted departed I got out the Brown Betty, boiled the water, threw in a couple of tea bags while Earl organized the tray and spoke, "Darling, it's long past time for me to explain about my, uh, hearing problems. Let's move into the living room for a refreshing couple of tea. Do you have the ginger snaps I baked yesterday?"

Grinning, he replied, "And our cups and our saucers and a couple of scones and the jam. Oh, I forgot the butter."

"It won't take that long, Earl. We shouldn't, really. We've already had our dessert."

"Speak for yourself, Gracie, I always have room for more."

"That's true. Are you ready?"

Indeed he was, rubbing his hands together in anticipation. I started in right away, "I should have realized I had a hearing problem back when I was eleven years old and I thought that my friend had told me that her mother had had to have a wrist removed. I saw her mother a month after the operation, and was amazed at how skilfully she carried a platter with an angel cake on it in one hand and a full tea cup balanced on its saucer in the other. Actually, I was disappointed that she was wearing long sleeves because I was dying to see her scars!"

Seeing the smile on Earl's face gave me the giggles, and it was a few minutes before I could continue, but after taking a sip of tea I went on, "My friend's simple explanation was supposed to solve the mystery for me, 'She had a fake one put in right away after the original surgery, you see'. In those days we never uttered the forbidden 'C' word for the disease and it was months later that I learned her mother had breast cancer."

Oh, how Earl and I laughed when I told him that the children's favourite of my many gaffes went like this: "Mum, do you have any brown thread?"

"No, but I have white sliced in the fridge."

Santa arrives in a hot car

The sound of the TV woke Grace up at 6 am, upsetting her instantly. Burying her head under her pillow, she was peacefully drifting back to sleep when the word 'snow' startled her. There she was dreaming of sunny Muskoka summers when it started to snow, snow cross-legged in fact, coating the forest, the lake and the boathouse deck. Aye!

She bounced out of bed, not at all in the manner she was accustomed to, and rushed downstairs to the kitchen to find her husband staring at the tiny television thoroughly captivated – or was it 'frightened'? – by the Ontario weather forecast. "Earl, why the heck are you watching this? There is nothing you can do about the weather anyway." Guiltily, her husband backed away from her menacing finger. "You're hiding something, Earl Cummings. You can't fool me! You think I haven't noticed your odd behaviour, your mood swings, your obsession with weather forecasts?" Pointing her finger right in his face, she shouted, "Am I stupid?"

Crash! Down went Earl's cup hitting the saucer and spilling hot tea on his toast and his pajamas. "Grace, I'm the stupid one. I made a promise I don't want to keep." While Grace absent-mindedly sipped her tea, Earl turned back to the TV and stared, while scenes of snow filled the screen. "Snow on Tuesday, snow on Wednesday, snow on Thursday and much more on Friday. Damnation!" He yelled, shutting it off with unnecessary force.

"Careful, dear, you'll break the knob. Move out of the way while I clean up the mess." Earl's arms flew straight up in the air, a gesture that she deliberately ignored. "It is past mid-December; what did you expect? What's up with you anyway? You like winter weather."

"I do, but it has to stop soon, doesn't it?"

"But I love it, too, Earl, you know that!" Exasperation had crept into her voice and led her to stir her tea with such vigour that she splashed her wrist. "Ouch!" she yelped.

"It's just that," he mumbled, "well ah, we must get ready to deliver our presents to the kids soon, very soon."

"Don't worry, dear, Christmas is still two weeks away, besides I really have bought light things, you know, a few articles of clothing for the grown-ups that will be easy to mail if we can't take them ourselves. Let's see now," she got up and put her cup and saucer in the dishwasher, "we still have time to send everything by mail. We agreed we'd send cheques – I sent them last week – for

Liv and Jessie to buy gifts for the kids themselves anyway and, as I said, my stuff will be easy to mail. Not cheap, but easy. Mailing certainly costs less than driving a total of twenty hours to make the deliveries ourselves." Grace had kept on talking, unaware of her husband's discomfort.

"Once and for all, it is up to us to take all the gifts from here, including Sarah's and Matt's for their sisters and brother. I've made a commitment and it will be lovely to see all the children and grandchildren."

"It would, you bet! I wish they didn't live so far away." Her sigh was barely audible.

"At least we're lucky they don't live in BC or Newfoundland."

"Don't worry about this any longer, dear. I'll get the parcels in the mail in plenty of time to arrive there before Christmas. I promise. I've only a few things left to buy. I'll do it all today, in fact. Satisfied?"

"No!" Earl pounded his fists on the table.

"What's with you, Earl? For crying out loud, would you please calm down; you startled me."

"Oh, Gracie, I'm so sorry," he stuttered, throwing his arms around his wife. His enflamed cheeks instantly lost their colour. "It's just that I promised. Oh, well, I'll have to tell you sooner or later."

"Promised what and to whom? My dear, you *are* a sorry sight!"

"You will be a worse sight when I tell you what you and I are going to do for our precious grandsons, Liv's boys."

With relief restoring Grace's equilibrium she surprised her husband with one of her trademark rumbling laughs. "Oh, Earl, you tried, I'll give you that, but, sorry dear, you haven't scared me one bit. For goodness sake, what could possibly be so upsetting if it involves any of our grandkids, especially since Shayne and Will aren't even teenagers yet? I mean, we're not going on 'Fear Factor' with them, are we? Aye, I don't like that look on your face. Shoot, Earl, are we? Fess up right now, Buster."

"Well, fear does describe the emotion correctly. You'd better sit down, my love. Would you like another couple of tea, dear? Yours must be cold." He dashed to the sink to refill the kettle, opened a package of social tea cookies, arranged them on a plate and dumped their cold tea into the sink all the while keeping his back turned.

Meanwhile Grace had taken off her cardigan and fanned her face with it. Flopping into a chair, she stretched her legs straight out in front of her and leaned back.

Suddenly she stood up, "Earl Cummings, I thought I was the procrastinator in this household but you take the prize today. Get over here with that tea and tell me what you're so scared of. Anything to do with our grandsons has to be good, not terrifying. Jeepers!" Her chair jerked as she landed hard on it. "Ouch." Rubbing her bottom she looked up at Earl, "I'm waiting, dear."

"Right, Grace, you're right, of course. I promised Liv that we would take Matt's presents for the two young'uns personally. There's no other way. We can't put Matt's gifts in the mail so I, uh, volunteered. But you're not going to like it."

"Of course I'll like it, dear. I'd love to go and see all the kids anyway, weather providing. It's fun playing Santa every year."

"Yes, and I guess they'll have gifts for us to bring home as well. Phew, so you don't mind? Do you really think we can fit a trip to Bracebridge in with all we have to do between now and Christmas?"

"Earl, you made a promise to Matt and Liv and we'll have to keep it. It's that simple, but if worse comes to worse we'll use UPS or Purolator. No more worries. I'd better finish doing the cards. At least the shopping for everyone is nearly done. Have you finished the wrapping, dear?" Jumping up from her chair she headed for the stairs, "By the way, dear, what are we delivering: furniture, baked Alaska?"

A long pause ensued.

"A lizard and a snake. A gecko actually," he muttered as a forced smile distorted his face. "It's a spotted leopard gecko or some such thing."

With trembling lips, Grace spoke slowly, "You mean a lizard and a gecko – alive? I can live with that. I do like geckos." She'd latched on to the word. "That means no snake?" She pleaded. "Oh, Earl, you scared me so much." At that point her whole body had started to shake. "Don't you ever tease me like that again or you will live on a daily diet of tripe, parsnip and cod liver oil. Earl Cummings." Then she appoaced him, placed her hands on his shoulders and pushed him hard. With her nose practically touching his own, she continued. "Don't you dare do that to me again!"

Now it was his turn to shake. "Uh, Gracie," he stuttered.

"Don't you 'Gracie' me! I've heard enough of your announcements. What were you thinking? Boy, you gave me such a scare! I hate snakes and you know it. How we managed to raise a son to become a reptile enthusiast is beyond me."

"Herpetologist, actually. Uh-oh, sorry, Gracie."

"You're interrupting! This conversation is over," said Grace as she stomped out of the room slamming the door behind her, muttering, "The very thought has ruined my day."

Earl chased her, "Dearest, how can I explain when you're so contrary. Come back and we'll have another couple of tea and discuss this rationally."

"It would hardly be rational for me, terrified as I am of snakes, to sit in the car with a snake inside somewhere in the back, not even in the trunk. See what the mere suggestion has done to me? I'm going to have nightmares, I know it, and that's not something a couple of tea can fix." When she looked at her husband she realized that he was as frightened as she was, though not for the same reason of course, and she softened her voice. "My dear, I know you love our grandchildren, so do I. Watching you makes me realize, somehow, oh, dear, that you're hiding something. Out with it, chicken! You know my bark is worse than my bite."

After clearing his throat, he proceeded to explain, "In the first place, a gecko is a kind of lizard. You know what that means? You do understand, don't you? The snake will be in a secure plastic terrarium with a few pinholes in it for air and the lid fits snugly. Matt will further secure the lid with a couple of bungee cords. We'll never have to open it."

"I'd rather go bungee jumping!" Reaching for a cookie, she replied with a trace of a smile, "What kind of snake is it? How long? Oh, never mind, spare me the details. I don't need them." Her cookie dropped from her shaky hand on to the carpet. "Uppsydaisy!" she uttered.

Tenderly taking her hands and enfolding them inside his, Earl continued, "There's more, Gracie. Matt and I discussed this and we've decided that it would be best if the snake and the gecko in their containers spend the night here before we leave, so that we can get an early start for Bracebridge. I'd like to get there before dark, and you know what Algonquin Park is like in the winter with twice as much snow as anywhere else on the route. It can be a nightmare."

"That's okay, I love the park. It will be very pretty. See, Earl, I'm trying to act like a grown-up. But where will the snake sleep in our house? Not in the guestroom, surely – I mean that's awfully close to our bedroom!"

"He'll stay in the downstairs bathroom, as it's the warmest room in the house. We won't be able to turn the heat down at all that night, by the way. Oh, dear, I suppose we'll have to keep the car warm, too. Matt suggested we put our hot water bottle under the containers and keep refilling it when necessary. He certainly didn't seem worried, but said 'absolutely not' to the critters' travelling in the trunk of the car."

"I already figured that out, dear. It would be terrible to arrive in Bracebridge with a pair of dead critters for the two little boys. Jeepers, it means we'll be sleeping in their house for two more nights with them – the critters, I mean. Earl, I don't know if I trust the boys not to let the snake out. It would escape for sure." Gritting her teeth she told her husband, "We'll just spend one night there and we'll seal our bedroom door. But even in the daytime if the snake gets loose in the house – ooh, it will be scary. Why are you laughing, Earl?"

"Relax, dear. These are Christmas presents, remember? The boys will know nothing about this till Christmas morning, when we'll be long gone. Liv will hide them at her office in town. It's already arranged. When we arrive she's going to take us there ostensibly to show us some of her latest kitchen design displays."

"Another trip with the snake?"

"Afraid so, dear."

"Any other surprises?"

"Trust me, none that I know of, other than the contents of all the gifts we'll be receiving."

"Good surprises, I'm sure."

"Of course," Earl replied giving Grace a quick hug. "It will be fun."

The night before the journey was not all that much fun for Grace, as she worried about the little gecko and snake and got little sleep. Twice she changed the water in the hot water bottle. Each time she felt thankful that the plastic containers were opaque.

The five-hour drive to Bracebridge became a six-hour endurance test because of the extra long stops for hot-water-bottle filling and a few snow squalls. The journey was not without its adventures. For one thing they made more gas stops than usual in order to keep refilling the hot water bottle. They were both paranoid about accidentally killing the critters en route. Furthermore, Earl kept jacking up the heat inside the car thus giving Grace a headache and dry, cracking lips. After about one and a half hours of driving, not yet in Ottawa, Earl complained of feeling sleepy.

Luckily he had a thermos full of coffee, but the consequences of so much coffee consumption necessitated extra comfort stops (as they called them), and furthermore probably contributed to his weird attack of dizziness when he got out of the car to fill the gas tank. Or was it the heat? At Grace's suggestion he turned down the speed of the fan to reduce the thrust of the Sahara blasts, that perhaps were doing harm to the snake and gecko as well anyway.

Much later when Grace was telling Matt about their journey, he would tell them they'd gone way overboard to protect his presents! To add fuel to the fire, a deer came from out of nowhere and bounded directly in front of their speeding car.

They'd have hit it had Grace not shrieked the moment she spotted it coming out of the ditch on Earl's side, thus prompting him to brake suddenly. A dangerous move itself in winter conditions, but one that saved the deer's life, and their lives. For once Earl praised Grace for her alarming scream, and Matt agreed with his father.

Perhaps their worst surprise was the discovery that they had left their packed lunch back home sitting in the fridge. Rather than take a long stop at a highway restaurant, they survived on the snacks they always brought with them for long trips. As Grace declared, making the best of things as usual, "It's a good thing I put some clementines in with the Doritos and chips. Do I ever have a thirst!"

"Me, too. We can't complain really, Gracie. At least we haven't had to put up with freezing rain or traffic tie-ups or police cars."

She nodded, "True. Heck, Earl, why didn't I notice our lunch when I pulled out the smoked meat and bagels? It's a good thing I didn't forget *them*. The kids would never forgive us if we arrived without their favourite Quebec foods. Oh, my!"

"Grace, you realize we'll be missing 'CSI' tonight."

"Oh, Earl, I get so annoyed with that show. Why do they always film murder scenes in the dark? And furthermore, why on earth don't they turn on the lights, at least while inspecting crime scenes? All their flashlights need new batteries. Anyway, it isn't logical unless they're outside in a deserted area at night. Come to think of it, why must all the murders and investigations happen at night, anyway?" Huffing, she shifted her position. "Boy, the car is hot! I hope 'Sneaky' and 'Lizzie' aren't suffocating."

"Do you want to lift the lids and take a look?"

"Ha ha," with a sigh of relief she changed the subject, "Two kilometers to Bracebridge, ah good."

A few minutes later, the hot, happy, hungry couple arrived at their destination and received a joyful welcome by their daughter, son-in-law, grandchildren, two dogs, and a turtle.

Time to take
Ernest Hemingway to bed

Once upon a time I tried to give you a graceful how-to for grandparenting. Well, now it's time to learn something more. But don't kid yourself, if you're not yet old enough to be a grandparent, then this new, gentle approach to aging is not for you. You can read it, but be sure to put on your rose-coloured glasses, or better still, the darkest sunglasses you can lay your hands on, thus ensuring you're not surprised by what lies ahead.

Notice how I refrain from such practicalities as specifying the age about which I am raging – Oh, pardon me, I meant to say 'alluding'. There is an explanation for my apparent memory loss and age has nothing to do with it, as far as I know. It's just that, um, what was I going to say? Excuse me while I give myself a caffeine boost, better known as 'Kicking Horse C.O.F.F.E.E'.

Wow, there's nothing like a gorgeous-tasting jolt of java. Makes me feel like a bucking buckaroo. Oh, the energy and the power! Do I sound like an addict? So what? Now I know what I was going to say (thanks to that ride on a kicking horse.) Phew. It is important. You're as old or young as you think you are, no more and no less. I ought to know because when you find out the rigmarole of activities I have to go through before going to bed and when getting up in the morning, you won't believe how young – sorry, just a Freudian slip – old I really am, either.

You see, the whole time I sit at my computer composing this little fact-of-life reminder involving countless annoying tiny tasks that keep me young-and-able, I'm actually daydreaming about Muskoka. Why? Well spring is here, and that means remembering that annual first visit up to the cottage every year for the 'May Weekend', the one that's labour intensive when we open the cottage after its long winter of sleep and decadence. That's right, I'm only remembering, not planning, because this year we don't have a cottage to make that first visit to any more, so we don't have to stock up on black fly spray, twenty-two chickens, bagels, and smoked meat from Quebec, mouse traps, sun screen, and fireworks.

Just remembering puts me in a terrific mood. Besides, we're coming back to Muskoka as renters anyway.

But I am rambling. That's one thing older people tend to do, and they are masters at procrastination for it takes years of practice to perfect it. I mean, like, you know, um, well I could bake a cake, clean house, weed the garden all in a flash when what I really want to do is, well, maybe, you know, is to write a newspaper column.

It's amazing the amount of work I can avoid by simply telling Earl, or myself, "I have to figure out the menus." It was by far my most frequently used and believed excuse all those years when we would be preparing for the arrival of family and friends for three-day to three-week visits at the cottage.

Now I have no excuse to use that excuse any more. Oh, well, I can always say I have to knit for the grandchildren because I love doing that and there are lots of little ones, including a great grandson – imagine that – who would just love yet another scarf or pair of mittens, I'm sure. The oldest grandchild is now twenty-four and doesn't fancy a hand-knitted scarf, nor does my next one, fourteen-year-old Cole.

When you grow older, you forget things. But you *never* forget Muskoka sunsets, the smell of lichens baking on pink-tinged rocks, the cry of loons, the sound of boats rocking in their slips on windy nights, or the magic that is a family of ducks floating by the dock sometimes with as many as ten or fifteen ducklings following behind. And how could you ever forget the feeling of a Muskoka lake's silkiness caressing you when you go for a skinny dip – and the adrenaline rush you get when you just might get caught in your birthday suit! These are the important things in life.

Did I say you forget things? I haven't forgotten – I've just been procrastinating. All along I've been meaning to tell you about getting ready for bed, and I promise not to leave out a single, silly detail.

So here's the routine, above and beyond the everyday stuff like washing and brushing teeth, undressing and putting on night clothes and putting moisturizer on flaky skin, turning down the heat and locking the doors. I take my pills with a large glass of water to jolly them along to their destination; remove that little donut thing I wear on the sole of one foot so that my callous doesn't hurt when I walk; remove the toe-separators I use to prevent my baby toe from sliding under my foot when I walk and the other separator that keeps my big toe from rubbing the toe next to it causing an itchy rash; take out my partial, brush it with toothpaste and leave it to soak in water and vinegar; take out both hearing aids, remove their batteries thus giving them a longer life. Then I'll do a few jumping jacks to prove I'm still an athlete; strap on my wrist supports to prevent my carpal-tunnel-syndrome-produced pinging hands, fingers and thumbs; put on my distance glasses if I'm going to watch TV in bed; or else I put on my reading glasses for obvious reasons, such as taking Ernest Hemingway to bed with me and going *Across the River and into the Trees* in Venice where *The Sun Also Rises* and *For Whom the Bell Tolls* makes me sad, and in the news we wish for a *Farewell to Arms,* and I will picture *The Hills of Kilimanjaro.*

Maybe I'll even dream that Earl is *The Old Man and the Sea,* and he nearly was when he caught his gigantic Northern Pike a few years ago. If, after I try to fall asleep (a huge challenge) I have an attack of the infamous 'restless legs syndrome', I'll get up and try walking it off. If that fails I'll have to take a pill that contains quinine (without the gin).

The next morning I reverse most of the steps I took the night before, and then I can have my first (and last) cup of coffee of the day – oh, joy! I'll take a different set of pills, chew a few prunes, have some bran, some Metamucil, then have breakfast that seems like an afterthought, but isn't, because that one piece of toast, white margarine and marmalade are pure ambrosia.

Don't worry, be happy, at least I don't have to put teeth in a glass of water or take out a glass eye or put a peg leg in the corner (as the song goes).

The Kicking Horse has kicked in. I'm ready to write another column, but I'll save that for another time.

What I dearly hope is that you get my point: that you are the age you think you are, more or less. Perhaps with a little help from the medicine chest and roasted black coffee beans from Brazil.

One more time

As I listen to Anne Murray crooning 'Old Cape Cod', I remember the unusual adventure I instigated last summer during my stay at my cousin's cottage, a place where I used to spend every summer of my youth mostly in or on the lake. I grew up skinny dipping every morning in the company of all the female family members and guests, young or old, spry or infirm, swimmers or non-swimmers.

You had to take that cleansing, frisky dip either wading deep enough to immerse your whole body except your head, or you could submerge yourself completely. You had no choice except when suffering from your monthlies. Heck, not having a clue what 'monthlies' or 'the curse' were when I was five years old,

I announced with disdain to one and all at the breakfast table that cousin Kay had skipped the dip altogether and for no good reason.

Immediately after breakfast, my mother taught me one horrifying yet fascinating fact of life. All that blood? Jeepers.

About the skinny dipping ritual there is more. One of my aunties had the strangest figure, quite unlike all the other developing or developed females'. Her chest was absolutely flat and the skin was blotchy with purple veins worming in all directions. It scared me so much that I didn't dare point it out to the unobservant entourage, nor did I ever ask even my mum about the ugly sight.

What I loved about the early morning swim was threefold: 1) The smell of the Ivory soap and the sight of it floating miraculously beside me as I did what we all did, much to the detriment of the lake. As you know, kids would prefer to skip washing themselves unless playing in the bathtub, and I was no exception. But doing it in Lake Rosseau was fun; 2) That silky feeling of the water caressing my naked body when I almost believed I was a dolphin; 3) At the first sign of a boat, the adrenaline's pumping through all our systems as we scrambled either under water or laid down in the scratchy blueberry bushes on land, or hastily swathed ourselves in our towels, often one-eighth the size of today's bath towels!

There were not many boats with noisy motors to warn you around my aunt and uncle's property, named Norway Point. Sundays gave the greatest challenge, for worshippers came by boat – we called it the 'church parade' – passing our swimming spot to attend Mass at the church about a mile across the water from us.

You can be sure that neighbouring cottagers, and probably a few mainlanders as well, knew about the Norway Point ritual.

The place name came, I thought, from the Norway pine tree that grows right at the northern tip of their land, where we always skinny dipped. As it was far enough from the main cottage, the point was considered safe from the eyes of the male guests, uncles, brothers, and cousins. If they did spy on us, we never knew. We certainly didn't spy on them when they had their turn every morning right after ours!

I have always romanticized about Norway and used to read about it, tried to learn the language, cycled there in 1950 and revisited it once again with all my family. Now I wonder if my fascination stems from the name's association with my happy youth at Norway Point. After referring to *The Audubon Society Field Guide to North American Trees* a few weeks ago, I discovered that the 'Norway' of the (red) pine refers to the Norway spruce tree that grows near Norway, Maine, – not even in Scandinavia! I was shattered. Aha! Imagine my excitement when Jenny informed me yesterday, that when her grandfather bought the Muskoka property it was already named Norway and the property across the bay was, of course, Sweden. Reinforcing my fascination, there was an air force base in Ontario called 'Little Norway' where Norwegian men trained as pilots during the war. Gee, I thought they were the handsomest creatures!

What woman doesn't idolize a Viking, for goodness sake!

But I have strayed, as I am wont to do. Last summer I watched my cousin Jenny as she walked carefully with the aid of an artistically decorated, gnarled wooden cane on the rough terrain that is

Muskoka. She was eighty-seven, seven years older than I, had just had a quadruple bypass, ending up with a cow's valve that was perhaps an upgrade from the pig's valve she was expecting, and had Parkinson's Disease. She was the last surviving member of her family of one brother and three sisters, my beloved cousins. Always blessed with more energy than I ever had, and with a good sense of humour, Jenny was great fun.

Watching her inspired me. In fact, a crazy idea popped into my head. To tell the truth, I was longing for a skinny dip, a pleasure I hadn't had since we sold our cottage. Skinny dips were no longer *de rigueur*, and I saw that very few of us elderly souls would be able to make it safely to the point anyway – better to swim off the dock nearby, wearing bathing suits, of course.

The walk from the cottage to the relatively private point is difficult for the best of us, with its rocky surface, scattered clumps of blueberry bushes and wintergreen and baby pines sprouting upwards here and there with roots snaking in the mossy soil. In Muskoka, I swear there is not one foot of level ground except where man in his madness has carved out golf courses, tennis courts and roads. I knew I could make it, however, but could Jenny? I realized that she, who, like me, adored being tomboyishly active and daring, probably hadn't been even close to the Norway pine in the last few years since suffering from serious health problems, let alone been able to indulge in a sinful dip in a lake, where fast-moving boats abound and slippery rocks render entering it well nigh impossible.

Did I say entering? What about getting out! I know that part of the shore like the proverbial palm of my hand. There were tiny inlets, some short trees and roots to grab and a couple of spots where the rocky ascent was gradual and which I could render less slippery with the use of a copper brush designed explicitly for my purpose. We all had such a tool at our cottages! Furthermore, since I had scouted the area the previous afternoon, I knew that we would together be able to get Jenny out of the water safely.

I am very strong and not afraid. Fortunately, Jenny trusted me so off we went, leaving the remaining guests to take their time getting up from their beds, take their turn in the one and only bathroom, and plug in the coffee machine that my cousin had set up the night before. Of course they wouldn't mind waiting for their breakfast until their hostess returned invigorated by an early morning skinny dip! They only had to wait an hour and a half, no big deal. Getting to the point wasn't too bad – it is somewhat downhill anyway.

Picture this: two old ladies on a mission to relive a rite of their youth. Two old ladies clambering and stumbling along the familiar rocky route from the cottage to the point. The older cousin sporting her cane about which she tends to brag, calling herself the "chick with a stick." The sun shining down on the Precambrian Shield with their pink-tinged rocks decorated with heavenly scented lichens. At the end of the trek because they are in full sun its rays resting passively on Jenny's pure white head and sparkling on the silver of Grace's hair. Jenny looking down because she doesn't want to fall. The disease has affected her balance but not her spirit.

Making quite a silhouette, this pair: Jenny straight and tall, Grace with her chin jutting out ahead of the rest of her body with its humped back and skinny legs. The picture becomes more interesting when they strip, revealing their white torsos, well-rounded bellies, shapeless buttocks, bony knees and hammer toes. You can tell they are blood relatives just from their shape, and they walk with feet turning way out, but ballet dancers they are not! Giving the appearance of camouflage, they both have arms and hands covered with dark bruises, turkey spots and Band-Aids they use to staunch the blood flow produced by their daily doses of baby Aspirin. Jenny's smile is much better than Grace's because her teeth are white. Whereas Grace's originals, those she still has that is, are a shade of dirty yellow, as if she had chewed tobacco all her life.

Actually, wanting to emulate famous baseball players, Grace once stole some of her older brother's pipe tobacco and tried chewing it. Well, like those baseball players she admired so much, she sure did manufacture a big ball of rusty brown spit and she never tried it again!

Getting into the water was okay, as Jenny sat on her bum and edged herself down the sloping rock and slid in. Since these were my old stomping grounds, I knew exactly where I could take a safe dive. Quick! I had to take my plunge now, a motor boat was heading our way! Yikes! Oh, ho, the memories, the adrenaline, the challenge and wow, the smooth, silky water! Starting with the breast stroke, if only that would restore our muscles, we spent a quarter of an hour practising all our strokes and swimming under water, as always with eyes wide open. Conversation was brief but our smiles were constant.

Too bad we had to get out. I crawled out of the water up the same ledge Jenny had used going in. After drying myself I explored the shore once more and chose a tiny, tiny bay a few feet away that was shallow and partly sheltered from the view of canoeists who might be slipping silently by. Well, Jenny was out of view as long as she was in the water but on land I wasn't, not when standing up anyway. Since I had to haul my cousin out of the water and up on to the land, I had to find a sapling or root to hang onto for support as I leaned over the edge to grasp her outstretched hand. I pulled and pulled while she pushed and pushed with her feet but we both giggled so much that we ran out of breath and strength. We searched for a better spot where I could more or less stand her up, support her steadily and practically piggyback her over the bank. It took several tries and several tumbles back into the lake and a whole lot of shrieks of laughter before I was able to haul my brave cousin on to dry land and into a sitting position.

While we rested I looked at her and realized what a picture we were. It was an amazing scene we were painting, with our wet hair plastered against our scalps displaying pink flesh and strips of grey and white hair. The highlight of the canvas, however, was the sagging breasts. Honestly, hers were practically tickling her navel and mine were bobbing near my sternum. Most of the time we spent bent over at the waist and, boy, did those hanging things swing like Hawaiian dancers, especially hers, as she was better endowed than I.

A couple of times we had to flatten ourselves so that we wouldn't be spotted. Each time it was hard work, but with more laughter we managed to get Jenny back up and balanced on her feet. On hands and knees, I scrambled to fetch our towels and clothes and her cane. Of course we were no longer as clean as we had been when we finished our swims, but who cares about a little mud and strands of water lilies tangled in our toes?

When eventually we reached the cottage we received a huge, if worried, welcome. Jenny couldn't have been happier about our return to that ridiculous rite of our youths. I loved every minute of it but suspect it would be the last time we'd be allowed to try such a silly stunt.

I am thankful I was able to share with her the gift of a skinny dip one more time.

Part 4

Twilight Tea:
Epilogue

Grace and Earl
enter their sunset years

"Earl, where are you? Yoo hoo!" Grace called, "Come have a look at the sunset. Hurry!"

Crawling out of the bathroom, Earl yelped, "I put my back out. Ouch, I can't get up!" As she lurched towards him he stretched out his arm at full length, "Don't touch me, Grace, please. Sorry, dear, I can't get up but I would like your help when I get to the – oh, where shall I sit?"

In a flash, Grace took command. "M'gosh, my love, can you make it on all fours to the living room? You're going to need a comfortable chair," she rubbed her chin, "but it can't be too soft. The one by the window would be the best, I think. Okay?"

She preceded him into the living room, and after rearranging the sturdy armchair so that her husband would have a good view of the street, she picked up a small table to put beside it. "Earl, what the heck were you doing? You know, this hasn't happened to you since you crawled into the house cursing and shouting, 'I'll never shovel snow again!' That's at least ten years ago, old man, and guess what, Earl Cummings, you kept your word, uh, more or less. And furthermore, you took me at my word when I told you that shovelling snow was my favourite winter activity."

"Ouch!"

Grace dashed forward and dropped to her hands and knees, "For Pete's sake, Earl, let me help you into the chair this minute! Hold still, my dear, while I guide your hands on to the seat of the chair. Slowly, one hand at a time, there now, hang on while I hold the chair down. Now pull yourself up. Can you do it?"

He did, but nearly tipped over before he finished turning himself around to sit down. Beads of sweat broke out on his forehead. "Just let me rest, Grace. I'll be okay. Phew, that was hard!"

"You sit tight, dear; I'll fetch the Aspirin. Need anything else?" Looking back over her shoulder, she wondered if perhaps he was going to milk the situation just the tiniest bit, and then shame overcame her, for she knew that it was what *she* might have done, but not Earl. She wanted to laugh at herself, but didn't dare. "What were you doing?" Shocked, she swung around, "Earl, you big lug, this isn't funny!" Wow, was he reading her mind? Jeepers!

"Aye, it hurts when I laugh but I can't help it; you won't believe me when I tell you what I was doing. Ha, ha, oh, dear, this is no time for hysterics."

"Well?" Her foot tapped the floor. "For crying out loud, Earl, you still haven't answered my question."

"I was shaving. That's all."

"You're kidding." It didn't take long for Grace's throaty chuckles to soar out of her wide-open mouth and turn into room-filling shrieks, snorts and sobs. Tears dribbled down her flushed cheeks. "That's impossible darling, c'mon – shaving?"

"It's no worse than the time you put your back out standing at the sink washing dishes. Remember?"

"How could I forget? You're right, dear. And I also haven't forgotten when it happened at the worst possible time, while I was doing up the long zipper of my kilt before serving Christmas dinner many years ago." She sighed. "I loved it when long kilts and dresses were in style back in the seventies."

A few minutes later she returned with the Aspirin and a glass of water along with *The Gazette*.

"Thanks, Gracie."

"Oh, before I forget, here's a bell for you. Try to rest, dear." Unfolding a brand new blanket and draping it over him, she lifted a corner where the label caught her attention. "Wow, Earl, listen to this, '100% unknown fabric'. Honestly," she giggled, "that's what it says. How reassuring is that!"

"Stop making me laugh."

"Oh, sorry, dear. Will you be okay while I finish making dinner? I have a good idea – maybe it will help take your mind off the pain if after dinner we talk about our trip."

"I'd like that, Gracie, and we can have a soothing couple of tea. I'll be fine. In fact I'm going to do some walking – it can't be as bad as sitting. Don't worry, I'll be careful."

"I agree. It's a good idea, but tonight you may find lying in bed pretty painful. My goodness, you may even have to sleep on the carpet beside the bed!"

"But, how would I ever get up off the floor? Forget that idea! And, Grace, it didn't help when you told me that the average age of the people on our seniors tour is *eighty-one*."

Laughing, she said, "Let me increase your misery, dear. Our tour leader informed me that she is always vastly relieved at the end of a trip if she can brag that nobody died!"

"Australia had better be beautiful, Gracie. Your new information has got me worried."

"Oh, you needn't worry about the older travellers. They're usually the most adventurous."

"Really?"

"Absolutely. They're so uninhibited. They're always delighted to show us young'uns," her eyes rolled, "Did I say young'uns? Anyway, they know how to have a good time, for sure."

With a smile of relief, he muttered, "Good, I think the Aspirin is working." Instantly, a frown appeared, "I hope the hotels there have proper pillows! Remember that time in Toronto when we discovered we had only feather pillows in our hotel room, and only one pillow each at that, and we ordered two foam ones to be sent up for me?"

"Oh, that was so funny. We couldn't go to bed because we were waiting for your pillows and finally at one in the morning a Spanish-speaking clerk appeared at the door with two razors and shaving foam. What did he think I was going to do, shave my legs at 1 a.m.? The poor guy, he probably had to go to an all-night pharmacy to buy the stuff in the first place. Did we ever laugh!"

"We sure did, and we couldn't get him to understand that I was allergic to feathers, so we had to wake up the hotel manager to have him take care of it."

"And he was not too pleased. Jeepers, we were already emotionally drained from 'The Phantom of the Opera', weren't we?"

He replied with a shrug, "Speak for yourself, Gracie. You would think that in this day and age, with allergies so rampant, that foam pillows would be the norm. Especially in a four-star hotel!"

"I bet they are in Australia, dear. You know," gently rubbing the back of Earl's head, the part that still retained hair, she continued, "Earl, what about our going back to Holland instead of Australia. It'd be almost like renewing our vows. As you can see, I've never taken off my engagement ring since I lost and luckily retrieved it, only hours after you put it on my finger at the diamond shop in Amsterdam. How many miles had we cycled when I realized I had left it in the restaurant's washroom?"

"That was when you nearly lost me, old girl!"

"And don't I know it. Shoot, I've never cycled so hard in all my life, and were we ever lucky!"

"*You* were lucky, you mean."

"I bet we'll find that generally the Dutch are as honest now as they were back then." Twisting the ring around her finger she shuddered. "I'd better get this ring made smaller; I can't lose it a second time. Aye-aye!"

"No you'd better not."

"I know what we'll do, we'll try to find that restaurant again. We'll even rent bikes!"

"Gracie, now you are getting carried away! Ahem, what about dinner?"

"Don't worry, I made a shepherd's pie this morning and all I have to do is reheat it in the microwave and I'll open a tin of corn to go with it."

"Don't forget the ketchup, Gracie."

"Boy! I wouldn't dare. You're enjoying yourself already, I see." His happy habit of rubbing his hands together had brought a sense of peace to the scene. "We'll have dinner and a couple of tea, and then I'll bring my old Dutch photo album, along with some travel brochures and your cheque book."

"What!" Earl jerked his head and winced.

Epilogue

Having entered a new era, a gentler post-working and post-cottage era, Grace and Earl found that they had more time for reminiscing. Enjoying a couple of tea, when they would remember, relax and recoup, enhanced their days more frequently than before.

Sharing their passion for gardening in their back yard in Pierrefonds, Earl tended his flowers, especially his Passion Flowers that spent winters staying alive in the basement under grow lights, and also his tomato plants, zucchinis and peppers. Meanwhile, Grace took care of her precious herbs, bedding plants and various rock displays including a couple of inukshuks, one in the front yard and one in the back under a big pine.

With more time to spare, Earl, having graduated from hot dogs and chips to experimenting with cooking, thrived on his wonderful Mediterranean, Chinese, Italian, and Japanese creations, as did Grace. Because they were anxious to keep their figures (a big challenge), Earl had to limit his marvellous baking production, or else give some of it away to the very happy Sarah and Matt. Alternatively, he could freeze it to take to Jack, Liv and Jessie and the grandchildren. Oh, yes, he continued to make his famous Christmas log, *quatre quarts*, *croquants* and chocolate-bourbon-pecan pies.

Grace's knitting became more prolific and complicated. Unfortunately, she knitted a V-neck, cable stitch sweater for Sarah (unlucky Sarah again), that was too small and she ended up giving it to Sarah's petite best friend. Always up for a challenge, she purchased the wool and pattern for an afghan that involved fourteen different kinds of stitches (for example: bramble, ballerina skirts, arrow ridge and shell pattern).

Although they spent more time travelling both abroad and in Canada to visit the children and grandchildren, they always loved coming back to their home in Pierrefonds, where sleeping in their Queen-sized bed – and indulging in a couple of tea remained as comforting as ever.

Acknowledgements

I'll always be grateful to Dr. Cohen, my English teacher in my final year at Toronto's Havergal College for her great grammatical guidance.

During my writing journey, I've had quite a few helpful editors, notably Brenda O'Farrell and Hollie Watson of Montreal's West Island weekly newspaper *The Chronicle*, which actually paid me for my articles and children's stories.

Their encouragement gave me enough confidence to take risks when writing and submitting instead of humbly experimenting with "safe" subjects and styles.

If it weren't for Iris Wallace of Wallace Marine, I probably would never have tried to write for the *Muskoka Sun*. Oh the discussions she and I indulged in, each with our own ambitions!

Soon after my husband and I bought our property on Lake Rosseau's Tobin Island, Dave Opavsky came into my life as the new editor of the *Muskoka Sun*.* Thanks to him, I became 'The Backwards Boater', a regular columnist for the *Muskoka Sun*, where I toiled for sixteen very happy years. Dave is my hero, allowing me to choose my own topics, of course always related to Muskoka. He encouraged me and used to send me timely, short, funny emails, which naturally made me want to laugh as well as write properly and promptly. I've kept those emails; they are treasures.

A confidence booster came from dear friends – and cousins sort of – Wendy and Matthew Stow, who have a cottage at Port Sandfield in Muskoka. They always read the columns and took the trouble to make good comments about them. A bit of back patting never hurts and I thank them.

As a member of the West Island Writers Group, I've learned much about the writer's craft and received excellent feedback from all its members. They have kept me on my toes and egged me on. It has been an enjoyable experience contributing to our three anthologies.** The launches for these anthologies were uplifting! I thank them for listening to enough parts of *A Couple of Tea* to lead me to finish the manuscript and submit it for publication.

I am grateful to Judith Isherwood, publisher of Shoreline, whose positive response is the fulfillment of my forty-four-year-old dream. At Shoreline I now have another wonderful editor, Paul Taylor, who has certainly helped bring *A Couple of Tea* into shape.

Writing and preparing *A Couple of Tea* for publication has been an education and the experience of a lifetime.

* A good share of the content of *A Couple of Tea* was originally published in the *Muskoka Sun* in the weekly 'Backwards Boater' columns from 1992-2008.

** "The Best Gift" was originally published in the West Island Writers Group anthology Winter Memories, 2005, published by Shoreline.

About Ann Benattar

Born in Toronto, Ontario, July 15, 1927, Ann Hamilton Boswell attended Havergal College for eleven years, graduating in 1946. She spent three years at the University of Toronto earning her Honours Bachelor of Arts degree. After exploring Europe and working in London's Trafalgar Square for eighteen months, she returned to Toronto.

She married Henry Benattar, whom she had met at the National Union of Students Hostel in London's Bloomsbury district. They took up residence in Montreal, ending up four years later in their own house in Pierrefonds, where they enjoyed raising their family of five children. From 1980 until 2004 she and Henry were owners of a piece of land on Muskoka's Tobin Island in Lake Rosseau, providing a place for their family and friends to enjoy many happy summers.